Yuming's *The 14th Moon*

33 1/3 Global

33 1/3 Global, a series related to but independent from **33 1/3**, takes the format of the original series of short, music-based books and brings the focus to music throughout the world. With initial volumes focusing on Japanese and Brazilian music, the series will also include volumes on the popular music of Australia/Oceania, Europe, Africa, the Middle East, and more.

33 1/3 Japan

Series Editor: Noriko Manabe

Spanning a range of artists and genres—from the 1970s' rock of Happy End to technopop band Yellow Magic Orchestra, the Shibuya-kei of Cornelius, classic anime series *Cowboy Bebop*, J-Pop/EDM hybrid Perfume, and vocaloid star Hatsune Miku—33 1/3 Japan is a series devoted to in-depth examination of Japanese popular music of the twentieth and twenty-first centuries.

Published Titles:

Supercell's *Supercell* by Keisuke Yamada

Yoko Kanno's *Cowboy Bebop Soundtrack* by Rose Bridges

Perfume's *Game* by Patrick St. Michel

Cornelius's *Fantasma* by Martin Roberts

Joe Hisaishi's *My Neighbor Totoro: Soundtrack* by Kunio Hara

Shonen Knife's *Happy Hour* by Brooke McCorkle

Nenes' *Koza Dabasa* by Henry Johnson

Yuming's *The 14th Moon* by Lasse Lehtonen

Forthcoming Titles:

Yellow Magic Orchestra's *Yellow Magic Orchestra* by Toshiyuki Ohwada

Kōhaku utagassen: The Red and White Song Contest by Shelley Brunt

33 1/3 Brazil

Series Editor: Jason Stanyek

Covering the genres of samba, tropicália, rock, hip hop, forró, bossa nova, heavy metal, and funk, among others, 33 1/3 Brazil is a series devoted to in-depth examination of the most important Brazilian albums of the twentieth and twenty-first centuries.

Published Titles:

Caetano Veloso's *A Foreign Sound* by Barbara Browning

Tim Maia's *Tim Maia Racional Vols. 1 & 2* by Allen Thayer

João Gilberto and Stan Getz's *Getz/Gilberto* by Brian McCann

Gilberto Gil's *Refazenda* by Marc A. Hertzman

Dona Ivone Lara's *Sorriso Negro* by Mila Burns

Milton Nascimento and Lô Borges's *The Corner Club* by Jonathon Grasse

Racionais MCs' *Sobrevivendo no Inferno* by Derek Pardue

Naná Vasconcelos's *Saudades* by Daniel B. Sharp

Chico Buarque's *Chico Buarque* by Charles A. Perrone

Forthcoming Titles:

Jorge Ben Jor's *África Brasil* by Frederick J. Moehn

33 1/3 Europe

Series Editor: Fabian Holt

Spanning a range of artists and genres, 33 1/3 Europe offers engaging accounts of popular and culturally significant albums of Continental Europe and the North Atlantic from the twentieth and twenty-first centuries.

Published Titles:

Darkthrone's *A Blaze in the Northern Sky* by Ross Hagen

Ivo Papazov's *Balkanology* by Carol Silverman

Heiner Müller and Heiner Goebbels's *Wolokolamsker Chaussee* by Philip V. Bohlman

Modeselektor's *Happy Birthday!* by Sean Nye

Mercyful Fate's *Don't Break the Oath* by Henrik Marstal

Bea Playa's *I'll Be Your Plaything* by Anna Szemere and András Rónai

Various Artists' *DJs do Guetto* by Richard Elliott

Czesław Niemen's *Niemen Enigmatic* by Ewa Mazierska and Mariusz Gradowski

Forthcoming Titles:

Los Rodriguez's *Sin Documentos* by Fernán del Val and Héctor Fouce

Massada's *Astaganaga* by Lutgard Mutsaers

Nuovo Canzoniere Italiano's *Bella Ciao* by Jacopo Tomatis

Amália Rodrigues's *Amália at the Olympia* by Lilla Ellen Gray

Ardit Gjebrea's *Projekt Jon* by Nicholas Tochka

Vopli Vidopliassova's *Tantsi* by Maria Sonevytsky

Édith Piaf's *Recital 1961* by David Looseley

Iannis Xenakis' *Persepolis* by Aram Yardumian

33 1/3 Oceania

Series Editors: Jon Stratton (senior editor) and Jon Dale (specializing in books on albums from Aotearoa/New Zealand)

Spanning a range of artists and genres from Australian Indigenous artists to Maori and Pasifika artists, from Aotearoa/New Zealand noise music to Australian rock, and including music from Papua and other Pacific islands, 33 1/3 Oceania offers exciting accounts of albums that illustrate the wide range of music made in the Oceania region.

Published Titles:

John Farnham's *Whispering Jack* by Graeme Turner

The Church's *Starfish* by Chris Gibson

Forthcoming Titles:

Regurgitator's *Unit* by Lachlan Goold and Lauren Istvandity

Ed Kuepper's *Honey Steel's Gold* by John Encarnacao

Kylie Minogue's *Kylie* by Adrian Renzo and Liz Giuffre

Alastair Riddell's *Space Waltz* by Ian Chapman

The Dead C's *Clyma est mort* by Darren Jorgensen

Chain's *Toward the Blues* by Peter Beilharz

The Front Lawn's *Songs from the Front Lawn* by Matthew Bannister

Bic Runga's *The Drive* by Henry Johnson

Hilltop Hoods' *The Calling* by Dianne Rodger

Yuming's *The 14th Moon*

Lasse Lehtonen

Series Editor: Noriko Manabe

BLOOMSBURY ACADEMIC

NEW YORK · LONDON · OXFORD · NEW DELHI · SYDNEY

BLOOMSBURY ACADEMIC
Bloomsbury Publishing Inc
1385 Broadway, New York, NY 10018, USA
50 Bedford Square, London, WC1B 3DP, UK
29 Earlsfort Terrace, Dublin 2, Ireland

BLOOMSBURY, BLOOMSBURY ACADEMIC and the Diana logo are trademarks
of Bloomsbury Publishing Plc

First published in the United States of America 2022
Reprinted 2022

Library of Congress Cataloging-in-Publication Data
Names: Lehtonen, Lasse (Lasse Antti Johannes) author.
Title: The 14th moon / Lasse Lehtonen.
Description: [1st.] | New York : Bloomsbury Academic, 2022. |
Series: 33 1/3 Japan | Includes bibliographical references and index. |
Summary: "Yuming's fourth album, The 14th Moon (1976), is not only an iconic
landmark of Japanese popular music history but also a window to musical
and social change in 1970s Japan-especially from the viewpoint of female
musicians"– Provided by publisher.
Identifiers: LCCN 2021060117 (print) | LCCN 2021060118 (ebook) |
ISBN 9781501378126 (hardback) | ISBN 9781501378133 (paperback) |
ISBN 9781501378140 (epub) | ISBN 9781501378157 (pdf) |
ISBN 9781501378164
Subjects: LCSH: Matsutōya, Yumi, 1954–14th moon. |
Popular music–Japan–1971–1980–History and criticism.
Classification: LCC ML420.M336333 L45 2022 (print) |
LCC ML420.M336333 (ebook) | DDC 782.4216/30952–dc23
LC record available at https://lccn.loc.gov/2021060117
LC ebook record available at https://lccn.loc.gov/2021060118

ISBN: HB: 978-1-5013-7812-6
            PB: 978-1-5013-7813-3
          ePDF: 978-1-5013-7815-7
         eBook: 978-1-5013-7814-0

Series: 33⅓ Japan

Typeset by Integra Software Services Pvt. Ltd.
Printed and bound in Great Britain

To find out more about our authors and books visit www.bloomsbury.com
and sign up for our newsletters.

Contents

The 14th Moon

Preface

Japanese names are written in the Japanese order, family name first, except for those Japanese scholars who have published their work in English and use the Western order.

Yuming performed under her maiden name Arai Yumi before getting married and changing her name to Matsutōya Yumi in 1976. To not make things overly complicated, this book refers to her as "Yuming" (*Yūmin*)—the nickname by which she has been called by her fans and the media since her debut.

The English-language titles given for Yuming's songs and albums are those that have been officially approved by her own management company, Kirarasha (Mica Company). This convention is to facilitate identifying the songs, as these translations are used by streaming and other services. As other translations are certainly possible, the original Japanese-language title is given in parentheses upon the first mention of a song or album, except for songs whose original title is in English.

The spelling of Japanese words follows the modified Hepburn system. Macrons are added for long vowels (e.g., Matsutōya), except for Japanese words that have been adopted to English (e.g., Tokyo) and for titles where Kirarasha omits the macron (e.g., "Chuo Freeway").

Finally, all musical transcriptions, as well as translations from Japanese to English, are by the author, unless otherwise indicated.

Acknowledgments

I am indebted to countless colleagues, friends, and students for all the support and inspiration they have given to me while I was working on this book. First and foremost, I wish to thank the 33 1/3 Japan series editor, Noriko Manabe, for her invaluable insights, inspiring guidance, and rigorous improvement of my writing. Everyone at Bloomsbury has been very helpful during the process of preparing the publication. I thank the two anonymous reviewers for their extremely valuable comments and suggestions that helped me develop my ideas. I state my deepest gratitude to the Ella and Georg Ehrnrooth Foundation and the Alfred Kordelin Foundation for financially supporting my research.

This book was mostly written while I was a visiting researcher at the University of Tokyo. I thank Professor Hermann Gottschewski for granting me the invaluable opportunity and everyone in our research seminar for their views and comments on my work. During recent years, I have had the pleasure of engaging in countless fascinating discussions about Japanese popular music. I especially wish to thank Hagita Mitsuo, Okamura Takako, Terashima Tamiya, Nozawa Kanae, and Aotani Michiko for their insiders' viewpoints; Lauri Kitsnik, Ogawa Hiroshi, Saitō Kei, and Wajima Yūsuke for their academic insights; and Kobayashi Akira, Togō Masahiko, Takamiya Yumiko, Oka Mayuko and Daisuke, Fujino Keisuke, Kuniko Shimomura, Miika Pölkki, and Aleksi Järvelä for sharing their personal thoughts and impressions with me.

I thank my family and friends, who have always been very encouraging of my work. I especially wish to thank Piia Ylitalo and Sauli Herrala for being so supportive of me while I was working on this book. My most special thanks go to my wife, Kumi, for her unforgettable musical performances and continuous support.

Introduction

In any case, I take pride in the fact that both the title and the contents of this album, The 14th Moon, *[…] represent the current me almost one hundred percent.*

– YUMING (ARAI 1976B, 58)

When singer-songwriter Yuming made her debut in 1972, Japanese popular music embarked on a new era. Her unconventional chord progressions, stylistic variety, and poetic lyrics about fashionable city life contrasted with virtually everything that the Japanese audience had heard before. Paired with her elaborate sound production and idiosyncratic voice, Yuming's work was initially met with bewilderment—especially within the music industry, which found her songs exceedingly difficult to classify into pre-existing genre categories. This bewilderment, however, soon transformed into an avid enthusiasm that launched what is now known as the "first Yuming boom" in the mid-1970s: Yuming's rise to one of the most popular musicians and sought-after songwriters in Japan.

The impact of this boom was massive. Apart from her musical approach that was admired by audiences, critics, and musicians across genres, Yuming was credited for establishing the female singer-songwriter in Japan, having been recognized for her ability to bridge commercialism and artistic integrity.[1]

Yuming's ability to anticipate upcoming trends and speak to audiences of different generations has been sustained for many years since her debut. Her albums have ranked in the top ten on the Japanese Oricon chart for five consecutive decades, and she was the first Japanese artist whose studio album reached sales of two million copies.[2] Yuming has long been popular in Asia, and more recently, she has also gained fans in the West due to the use of her songs in Miyazaki Hayao's animations *Kiki's Delivery Service* (1989) and *The Wind Rises* (2013). It is no surprise, then, that Yuming is commonly considered a cultural icon and one of the most influential figures in Japanese popular music history.

This book explores Yuming's unique position and her impact on the Japanese popular-music world by examining her fourth studio album, *The 14th Moon* (1976). The album is now considered a classic of 1970s Japanese popular music, due to its exuberant stylistic variety and generic hybridity. Fusing polished pop and rock sounds with Caribbean rhythms and jazzy swing, *The 14th Moon* established as Yuming's trademark the negotiation of conventional genre barriers, which has also inspired many other musicians. The best-known track of the album, "Chuo Freeway," anticipated several characteristics of City Pop of the 1980s and J-pop of the 1990s, and it has become a lasting favorite of fans and critics alike. In addition to its status as a musical landmark, *The 14th Moon* also offers a point of entry to Yuming's work in the broader social context of the mid-1970s. Yuming's music and public image were emblematic of changes in contemporary Japan, ranging from economic growth to urbanization, but I especially want to highlight her role as a pioneering female singer-songwriter.

From this perspective, the decade of the 1970s is particularly fascinating. It witnessed the emergence of a women's liberation movement and the debuts of the first female singer-songwriters in Japan. In only a few years, both became major phenomena: just as Japan witnessed feminism rise as a prominent (albeit relatively brief) media trend, its music scene saw a parallel boom of female singer-songwriters, such as Yuming, Nakajima Miyuki, and Takeuchi Mariya. These two developments were not directly linked—female singer-songwriters typically did not engage directly with contemporary feminist discussions or seek to represent a shared "women's voice"—but the variety of their songs and their celebrity as creative artists marked a momentous change for the music industry, which had previously been dominated by male songwriters and producers. In this respect, female singer-songwriters embodied many goals of contemporary women's movements and echoed broader social discussions about women's positions in Japan.

In this book, I argue that *The 14th Moon* symbolized this broader change in Japanese popular music. Even though Yuming does not explicitly comment on gender issues in her lyrics, *The 14th Moon* participated in diversifying women's images in popular songs and negotiated new definitions of authenticity and authorship for female musicians. As we will see, Yuming provided alternatives to conventional portrayals of women in popular music and the mainstream media. In this, *The 14th Moon* allows us to consider the work and significance of contemporary Japanese women musicians at large.[3]

Although my focus is on Yuming and Japan, anyone familiar with female singer-songwriters in Europe and North

America is likely to recognize parallels with their careers. For example, Yuming's position as an immensely successful performer and songwriter resonates with the work of Carole King. Her negotiation of genre boundaries and complicated relationships with mass media recall the career of Joni Mitchell. Her unapologetic attitude and skillful manipulation of her image echo the stance of Carly Simon. But what also connect Yuming with her foreign counterparts are the issues she had to face as a female musician in the 1970s—especially the expectations related to career, marriage, and motherhood. Therefore, this book can also be read as a case study about the successes and challenges of female musicians globally.

The book is divided into six chapters. Chapter 1 provides the background to Yuming's career by introducing her rise to stardom and her position in Japanese popular music in the mid-1970s. Chapter 2 takes a closer look at *The 14th Moon* by discussing the album's sound and style, and analyzing recurrent themes in the lyrics. These are contextualized in developments in Japanese popular music and society in Chapter 3, which demonstrates how the sonic and commercial aspects of *The 14th Moon* resonated with the complexity of genre definitions and reflected broader social changes, such as urbanization and economic growth. Chapter 4 continues this discussion by addressing the position of women in contemporary Japan and relating Yuming's career and the emergence of female singer-songwriters to the rise of two types of feminisms in Japan in the 1970s. Based on these observations, Chapter 5 analyzes how the lyrics of *The 14th Moon* portray their heroines and addresses how the album constructed Yuming's brand of authenticity specifically as a female musician. Finally,

Chapter 6 discusses the album's legacy by contextualizing it in later developments in Japanese popular music. Through this discussion, I argue that *The 14th Moon* carried the promise of larger changes: it was the perfect soundtrack for a period of musical and social transformations.

1 Becoming Yuming

"I'm a genius." That's what I keep on saying here and there. The reason I'm a genius is that I've kept on saying so before my debut—from the time nobody really recognized me. As I've continued to say it this long, I guess that I really am a genius.

– YUMING (MATSUTŌYA 1984, 7)

The Japanese youth were crazy about rock in the late 1960s. Japanese rock inspired by the Beatles' Merseybeat sound, called "Group Sounds," had an aura of rebelliousness but came from the mainstream media industry (Bourdaghs 2012, 125–6). Although worried officials and parents were still debating whether or not the electric guitar was even a decent instrument, the young audience knew what it wanted, and it rushed in great numbers to listen to its favorite groups (Take 1999, 94–121).

Among the most enthusiastic fans was a girl in her early teens. While there was nothing unusual about a teenage girl going after her idols, many rock musicians later reminisced that she always seemed exceptionally serious about music. For example, she had a habit of chasing after her favorite musicians backstage and to restaurants where they hung out—not to present them with plush toys and candies, as was typical for female fans, but to analyze, with intense excitement, the styles of her favorite British and American groups. According to the rock icon Kamayatsu Hiroshi, even the most progressive musicians of the time were often unfamiliar with the foreign records she proudly introduced to them (Matsuki 2016, 127).

It was during one of these backstage discussions that Sy Chen, the Chinese-born bassist of the Tokyo-based group the Fingers, asked the girl what she wanted to become in the future. According to Chen, she unhesitatingly replied that she wanted to become famous. Chen told her that in Chinese, "famous" is pronounced *yǒumíng*. Since the word also resembled the girl's name, Chen insisted it would be the perfect nickname for her (Chen 2005, 31).

This is how the young Arai Yumi was first called Yuming (*Yūmin*). Neither she nor Chen could have imagined that in only a few years, the name would be recognized throughout Japan. When *The 14th Moon* was released in November 1976, the country was at the height of a Yuming boom: not only had her albums and singles occupied the highest positions on the Oricon chart but she had also become one of the most sought-after professional songwriters and a popular fashion icon idolized by young women. No wonder that a magazine article heralded her popularity as something beyond a passing trend: "[Yuming's popularity] is not merely about songs going in and out of style; it is already an *event*" (Shūkan gendai 1976, 168).

Unsurprisingly, *The 14th Moon* was one of the most anticipated releases of 1976. Based on its commercial success, the album lived up to expectations exceedingly well: it reached the top position in the weekly sales in 1976, but even more remarkably, it was the fourth most popular album of 1977. To better understand the album's position in Yuming's discography, let us review how the young girl idolizing rock bands rose to stardom.

The Road to *The 14th Moon*

Yuming was born in January 1954 as the third child to parents running a kimono fabric shop in Hachiōji, a city in the western part of Tokyo.[1] The Allied Occupation of Japan had ended less than two years earlier, and Japan was just entering a period of spectacular economic growth, which resulted in some of the most optimistic decades in modern Japanese history. Brought up in an affluent home that emphasized the educational importance of music and other arts, Yuming spent her childhood days daydreaming, painting, and practicing music. Apart from playing the piano and singing in a church choir, she also studied the *shamisen*, a three-stringed plucked Japanese instrument. Shamisen songs would later have a surprising influence on *The 14th Moon* (Matsutōya 1984, 12–16; 29–30; 100–1).

While being surrounded by different types of music, nothing in Yuming's childhood suggested that she would become a popular music star. Having been taught that "if music is not classical, it's not music at all," she rarely had much chance to hear popular music (Music Life 1974, 167). Therefore, when Yuming happened to hear Procol Harum's "A Whiter Shade of Pale" (1967) in her early teens, the impact was momentous: she later described the song's combination of baroque-style organ music with rock as "shocking" to hear. In the wake of this experience, Yuming started writing songs, learning the bass, hoarding rock records, and hanging out with Japanese rock musicians. All was in the hope of attaining her new dream of becoming a professional popular song composer (Katsura 1976, 82; Matsutōya 1984, 44).

What served as a prelude to the fulfillment of this dream was the Japanese premiere of *Hair* in Tokyo in late 1969. Starred by popular singers—such as Kahashi Katsumi, a widely idolized former member of the Group Sounds band the Tigers—the production received notable media coverage and attracted Yuming's attention. Also among the cast was Sy Chen, who had become close with Yuming and was well aware of her musical ambitions. Yuming asked Chen to hand Kahashi Katsumi a cassette tape with recordings of her songs, in the hope that Kahashi would become interested in her work (Matsuki 2016, 114). This strategy worked out miraculously well, as Kahashi was apparently impressed by what he heard. When planning his upcoming third solo album in early 1971, he decided to include one song by Yuming, with new lyrics written by himself (Matsuki 2016, 115). To Yuming's surprise, she received an invitation to attend the recording of her debut composition "Suddenly, Love… " (Ai wa totsuzen ni…)—a song she had written when she was just fourteen (Suzuki 1976, 56).

Selling one's songs to producers was not an easy task, especially for a minor, and it was by no means obvious that Yuming would be requested to write new songs. Luckily for Yuming, however, "Suddenly, Love… " caught the attention of the influential musician and producer, Murai Kunihiko. Murai was among the songwriters who contributed to Kahashi's album and was known for his well-established international connections and interest in musical trends in Europe and the United States (Matsuki 2016). Aspiring to "raise the quality of Japanese music to an international standard," Murai had founded the record and publishing company Alfa Music in 1969 and was constantly in search of new talent that could help him fulfill his mission (Murai 2018, 208).[2] After hearing "Suddenly, Love…" Murai felt that he had discovered the talent he had been looking for. Impressed by Yuming's melodies and chord progressions which he thought carried a fresh and "international" flavor, he did not hesitate to express his enthusiasm about Yuming's work:

> [H]er songs were very sophisticated. I thought she was a genius immediately after hearing them and wanted her to succeed as a songwriter. That's why I had her write a new song. (Matsuki 2016, 118)

Murai contacted the seventeen-year-old and asked her to work as a songwriter for Alfa Music. Yuming, who would never have thought that she could achieve her dream so quickly, agreed immediately. But what she did not anticipate was that she would soon debut as a singer herself. As Murai later reminisced:

> At that time, neither I nor Yuming herself thought that she would debut as a singer. However, since the style of her songs was so novel, the way of performing them must also be novel. […] When I listened to her tape again, I started to find her way of singing very attractive. (Matsuki 2016, 118–19)

At this time, Yuming had just begun her studies in fine arts at Tama Arts University in Tokyo, majoring in Japanese-style painting, and aspired to become a composer instead of a singer. However, she agreed to Murai's proposal, reasoning that singing might be the only way to get her music known to the world:

> [I]t was said that it would be very difficult to make one's name as a composer. This was around the time that Carole King was becoming popular, and I was told that I could get my songs out to the world by becoming a singer-songwriter. [...] I had no intention of singing myself but ended up doing so anyway. (Matsutōya 1984, 89)

Alfa Music released Yuming's debut single "No Reply Needed" (Henji wa iranai) in July 1972. The single never became a hit—the story goes that it sold only 300 copies—but Murai had taken a liking to Yuming's idiosyncratic voice and wanted to produce her debut album. At that time, Alfa Music had just finished constructing its recording studio, Studio A, which was inspired by the studios Murai had visited in Europe and the United States. Proudly marketed as "the modern Stradivarius of studios," Studio A was constructed to enable elaborate sound production of an international standard (Matsuki 2016, 131). Reasoning that Yuming's musical style would perfectly align with his goal of making Japanese music "more international," Murai decided that her debut album, *Vapor Trail* (Hikōkigumo, 1973), would become the first work recorded at Studio A.

Yuming wrote all the songs on *Vapor Trail* and accompanied herself on the piano, backed up by the studio band, Caramel Mama. This band was known as an extension of Happy End, the rock group that is commonly (albeit misleadingly) celebrated as the "starting point" of Japanese-language rock.[3] Murai was convinced that the group would not only be likely to understand Yuming's musical vision but also provide her debut with an aura of artistic integrity; after all, its members had always demonstrated extraordinary skill in popularizing almost any musical act they collaborated with (Bourdaghs 2012, 176). For example, the bassist of *Vapor Trail*, Hosono Haruomi, later became globally famous as a member of the Yellow Magic Orchestra—another notable musical act produced by Alfa Music.

Murai's assumptions hit the mark: today, Japanese music critics generally agree that *Vapor Trail* was an epoch-making album. To begin with, the lyrics touched upon themes that were rarely addressed in popular Japanese songs. For example, "Vapor Trail"—which Miyazaki Hayao later used in *The Wind Rises*—was inspired by the suicide of Yuming's classmate (Arai 1976a, 55).[4] Unlike the more straightforward social commentary by previous folk musicians, "Vapor Trail" portrayed death in a subtle, poetic language open to interpretation:

Chorus: Longing for the sky, soaring to the sky,
Her life is a vapor trail

Not only was this portrayal uncommon, but it was also backed up with a musical style that mixed influences from American and British rock and seemed excitingly fresh in contemporary Japan (Kirarasha 2003, 20–1). Music critic Take Hideki later described his initial bewilderment upon hearing Yuming's music:

Her chord progressions were completely different from
folk singer-songwriters. […] Her sound was European, and

it resembled the smooth movement of a paintbrush on a watercolor painting. Her dry voice did not rely on vibrato and was entirely different from female […] singers at that time. Not forgetting elegance, her music also carried a hip fashion sense that was bewildering. (Take 1999, 172)

One novel aspect about Yuming's music was that it put an extensive emphasis on keyboards. This not only differentiated her from earlier folk and rock musicians, who typically played electric or acoustic guitars, but also highlighted her innovative use of chords. "Vapor Trail" begins with a soothing chord progression that draws on Procol Harum's "A Whiter Shade of Pale" and J. S. Bach's Aria from the third orchestral suite in D major. Apart from emitting an aura of artistic ambition, the reassuring atmosphere also conflicts with the serious theme of the song and creates an intriguing contrast between the music and the lyrics (Bourdaghs 2012, 181–2). The chord progression of the chorus (Ex. 1.1) was considered so innovative that Matsutōya Masataka, the keyboardist of Caramel Mama, jocularly stated that he immediately wanted to marry the composer after hearing it (Take 1999, 171). This anecdote would not have been repeated so often, though, had Yuming and Matsutōya not actually started dating during the recordings (Matsutōya 1984; Matsutōya 2016).

Example 1.1 *The chorus of "Vapor Trail" (00:56–1:07). The use of B♭m7 in place of the more typical B♭7 has been considered especially innovative.*

Despite critical acclaim, however, *Vapor Trail* was not an immediate success. In fact, as the album is now almost unanimously recognized as a classic of Japanese popular music, it is all too easy to dismiss the obstacles that Yuming's early career encountered. To begin with, the recording of the album was a rocky process, to say the least (Matsutōya 1984, 92; Matsuki 2016, 136–40; Matsutōya 2016, 41–2). The studio producer, Ariga Tsuneo, demanded countless retakes of Yuming's vocal parts to the point that Yuming proclaimed that she would never sing again: "You know, I can't sing… I really hate singing. […] It only makes me feel frustrated" (Music Life 1974, 197). When the album was finally released in November 1973, its sales were far from satisfactory. Yuming's music did not fit into pre-existing genre categories, and especially the poetic language and unconventional themes of the lyrics were largely considered "difficult" (Tomisawa 1979, 199). Although critics generally praised the music, some criticized the album for projecting an unbalanced image of a novice singer assisted by the more experienced Caramel Mama (Matsuki 2016, 183).

Still convinced that Yuming would eventually win the hearts of the audience, Murai urged her to release new albums. The sales of *MISSLIM* (1974) and *Cobalt Hour* (1975) were indeed more promising. Both were again accompanied by Caramel Mama (which had by then changed its name to Tin Pan Alley) but experimented with a greater diversity of Anglo-American popular music styles than *Vapor Trail*. For example, *MISSLIM* featured the funky "I'm All Yours" (Anata dake no mono) and the doo-wop background vocals of "December Rain" (12-gatsu no ame), while *Cobalt Hour* adopted 1960s pop idioms in "Don't

Ask Me Anything" (Nanimo kikanaide) and "Lipstick Message" (Rūju no dengon).

Moreover, both albums had more complex arrangements, including acoustic instruments such as the flute, fiddle, and harp. This influenced the overall sound of the albums: whereas *Vapor Trail* sought to evoke the atmosphere of the live sessions that Murai had admired in studios in the United States, *MISSLIM* and *Cobalt Hour* established elaborate studio production as part of Yuming's trademark (Kirarasha 2003, 24; Matsuki 2016, 135). As social psychologist Yoshida Kaori later put it, the perfection in sound production, combined with Yuming's adoption of foreign musical styles and occasional use of English-language phrases, established her image as simultaneously "distant yet attainable" to Japanese audiences. She was more attainable than foreign musicians singing in English, but her music always incorporated an aspect of exciting cosmopolitanism (Yoshida 1977, 19).

These approaches helped to expand Yuming's audience, and catchy songs like "Lipstick Message" and "Embraced in Softness" (Yasashisa ni tsutsumareta nara) found their way to the Oricon list as singles. Among Yuming's new fans was also Miyazaki Hayao, who was so fond of her songs that he would later listen to them all day long while working on his animations at Studio Ghibli (Suzuki & Matsutōya 2013, 52). This fondness can be witnessed in the use of "Lipstick Message" and "Embraced in Softness" in *Kiki's Delivery Service*; according to producer Suzuki Toshio, the songs became so important for defining the story's atmosphere that the film "could not even have been completed without them" (Suzuki & Matsutōya 2013, 53). Apart from fans, Yuming's albums were also applauded by music critics. Ogura Eiji from the *New Music Magazine* ranked *MISSLIM* as his favorite album of the year—a notable recognition at a time when most Japanese music critics usually preferred albums by Anglo-American artists (Matsuki 2016, 183).

What ultimately guided Yuming to her national breakthrough, however, was television. In 1975, she was commissioned to write the theme song for the drama *Family Secrets* (Katei no himitsu), whose producer was fond of *Vapor Trail*. The song, "Those Were the Days" (Ano hi ni kaeritai), became the best-selling single of the year, despite having been released as late as October. As Murai had anticipated, Yuming only needed one hit to rise to stardom: after the success of "Those Were the Days," all her previous releases occupied the top positions on the Oricon chart in an instant, which made her a celebrity idolized across Japan (Matsuki 2016, 206–7). By 1976, she had fully claimed the nickname Sy Chen gave her years earlier.

Release of *The 14th Moon*

The year 1976 turned out to be extremely hectic for Yuming. She released the single "The Paled Room" (Kageriyuku heya, 1976) in March and was constantly requested to write songs for various television programs. After the folk group Banban's "'Strawberry Statement,' Once More" ("Ichigo hakusho" o mō ichido) hit the sales charts in fall 1975, she had also become one of the most sought-after songwriters in Japan, which resulted in an enormous number of commissions from such popular singers as Agnes Chan, Gō Hiromi, and Ōta Hiromi.

At the same time, Yuming gave a nationwide concert tour from March to May, after which her first best-of album, *Yuming BRAND*, was released in June. Known as a witty speaker, she was also a popular guest on radio programs, and having become a fashion icon of sorts for young women, she constantly appeared on the pages of magazines like *Seventeen*.

And then there was her private life. She had to complete her graduation painting for the Tama Arts University during the spring, and having gotten engaged to Matsutōya Masataka in late 1975, she was busy planning her wedding. Their wedding, which became a widely covered media sensation, took place in late November—less than two weeks after the release of *The 14th Moon*.

In other words, *The 14th Moon* was produced under exceptional circumstances and carried enormous expectations. As a producer at Toshiba EMI stated:

> Yuming's charm lies in the way she skillfully matches the nice, watercolor-like touch of her poems with intense contrasts and beautiful melody lines. She has the talent of absorbing any kind of influence and making it her own. One can expect a lot from her upcoming LP. (Shūkan heibon 1976, 44)

To meet such high expectations, Yuming temporarily reduced all of her other works before the recordings of *The 14th Moon*, which were completed over a few days in September and October 1976 at Studio A (Matsutōya 2016, 74–6). An extremely contracted process compared with Yuming's earlier albums, all of which had taken over a month to record, *The 14th Moon* demonstrated that Yuming and her team had established a smooth routine even while producing her albums with meticulous attention to detail (Matsuki 2016, 136–40). As Yuming explained, everything that had happened after the release of *Cobalt Hour* had given her "an education worth five years" (Arai 1976b, 57).

The 14th Moon was the first album on which Yuming was not backed up by Tin Pan Alley, due to difficulties in matching everyone's schedules.[5] Although originally fretting about the unexpected situation, Matsutōya Masataka, who was now responsible for the production, managed to turn it around by assembling a group of experienced musicians and rising stars. To begin with, the background vocals were sung by Ōnuki Taeko, Ozaki Amii, Yamashita Tatsurō, and Yoshida Minako, all of whom later embarked on successful solo careers. Furthermore, many of the studio musicians were already highly experienced both within Japan and internationally. The guitarist, Seto Ryūsuke, had enjoyed moderate success in the United States with his rock group EAST in the early 1970s, and it was thanks to his connections that *The 14th Moon* also marked Yuming's first collaboration with prominent foreign musicians—Leland Sklar on bass and Mike Baird on drums (Matsutōya 2016, 74).[6]

With the new studio band, the general sound of *The 14th Moon* turned out differently from Yuming's earlier albums. Gone were the days when Yuming had been criticized as a novice singer "assisted" by a more experienced band: on *The 14th Moon*, it was Yuming who was clearly highlighted as the center of attention. The album perhaps evoked her flashy and action-packed concerts that subverted the traditional image of a modestly dressed singer-songwriter with her flamboyant fashion, backup dancers, and versatile stage props (Matsutōya

2011, 17; Yanagisawa 2011, 204). Music journalist Yuasa Manabu has in fact argued that *The 14th Moon* symbolized Yuming's growing self-confidence in her vision, even when it conflicted with the conventions of the music industry (Kirarasha 2003, 33).

But above all, *The 14th Moon* became an important watershed between what is now called Yuming's "Arai" and "Matsutōya" periods. While incorporating the polished sound and sensitive lyrics that had become her trademarks since her debut, the album also entailed important transformations. These transformations symbolized more than the development of one individual singer: they were also indicative of larger changes in Japanese popular music and society. To start unraveling this aspect, let us examine the music and lyrics of the album.

2 Transient Worlds

When I encounter something beautiful and wonderful, it makes me go, "Ah!" That's the emotion I want to share and transmit. That's why I write songs.

– YUMING (SEVENTEEN 1981, 53)

Listening to *The 14th Moon* can evoke a peculiar feeling. At first, it feels natural to focus on the melodies, rhythms, lyrics, and general soundscape—something one would do with any music. But as one listens further to the album, something strange begins to happen. It feels as if the music gradually wraps the surrounding reality in a dream-like fantasy, absorbing everything into its world. Yuming had a simple explanation for this phenomenon, arguing that her work is "background music" (Suzuki 1976, 57). But if this is the case, her music seems to immerse everything into that background.

This phenomenon has been explained in various ways. The social psychologist Yoshida Kaori has observed that Yuming's music renders everyday life into a dream-like reality that seems distant yet attainable at the same time (Yoshida 1977, 17). This carefully constructed balance in Yuming's songs has been characterized as "stylish" (*oshare*) and "city" (*tokaiteki*) (Sakai 2013). But while being true to a "light and sophisticated" sound (Stevens 2008, 47), Yuming's songs have never been "afraid to suggest an existentialist confrontation with darker possibilities"

(Bourdaghs 2012, 181). By incorporating this interplay of contrasts, her music seems to embody a world of its own.

While these characterizations apply to several Yuming albums, *The 14th Moon* takes this effect to the fullest through its variety of musical styles and its lyrics that are open to interpretation. The strange thing about this impression is that each track on *The 14th Moon* seems too independent to function as part of a unified reality; the album curiously celebrates singularity and plurality at the same time. How does it generate this immersiveness that has been experienced by so many listeners? Or is it all just in our imagination?

A Celebration of Musical Variety

The cover of *The 14th Moon* is tempting. Instead of the artist herself—the most common theme of album art for female singers in the mid-1970s—it depicts an LP wrapped in pink gift-wrap paper. Tied with a prominent red ribbon and sporting a gift card with "The 14th Moon from Yuming" printed in English, the cover carries the promise of an intimate gift. One can only try to imagine what it felt like to get one's hands on this long-awaited album in 1976: it was a symbolic present from Yuming to her fans who had so eagerly anticipated its release.

The aspect of intimacy is further enhanced by an accompanying four-page photograph collection of Yuming. Taken by Nagahama Osamu, the collection depicts her in diverse attire that plays with intriguing contrasts. We see Yuming dressed as an aviator and sitting on a stylish antique sofa wearing an extravagant fur coat—both situations that are clearly not part of everyday life and staged for photographs. But we also get glimpses of a casually dressed Yuming in outdoor settings in two photographs that look so natural that they could have been taken from her everyday life. A contrast between these photographs is constructed with a classic device: gaze. The everyday Yuming seems completely unaware of the camera; it is almost as if she were captured on the film accidentally (which adds to the photographs an aspect of intimacy). But in the two other photos, she demandingly looks back at the viewer—an effect that underlines the staged nature of the photographs (cf. Machin 2010, 39–42). By these contrasts, the photograph collection engages with the same interplay of dream-like fantasies and everyday life as her music, indeed rendering the artist herself "distant yet attainable." This impression also contributed to constructing Yuming's image as a cool and smart fashion icon, which had become an important part of her artist brand (Tomisawa 1979, 199–200).[1]

Placing the record on the turntable, one soon notices that it wraps up ten individual presents—that is, ten musically distinct tracks. While the general sound is relatively light, the stylistic variety draws intriguing musical contrasts, experimenting with different styles from jazz and Caribbean to rock and fusion. No wonder Yuming jokingly deemed her musical influences as "chaotic" (Katsura 1976, 82)! She also stated in retrospect that while each song on *The 14th Moon* feels complete in itself, the album lacks cohesion as a whole—or as she put it, a feeling of "totality" (Matsutoya 1984, 116).

However, I would argue that it is precisely the variety *within* the album that constitutes its musical backbone. Hagita Mitsuo—one of the most prolific popular music arrangers in Japan—has compared the task of an arranger to that of a cook. As Hagita explains, both professions are connected by an aspiration to create as attractive a result as possible from the given raw materials and instructions (Hagita 2018). Building on this metaphor, *The 14th Moon* best compares with a multi-course meal: with so much variation, the listener never gets tired of its musical narrative.

As with Yuming's two previous albums, the task of the "cook" was assumed by Matsutōya Masataka. By the time the album was produced, the couple had developed a routine for their musical collaboration: after Yuming had written the lyrics, melody, and chords, Masataka completed the arrangement. Although Masataka was known for experimenting with different styles while preparing his arrangements (he originally arranged "Those Were the Days" as a country tune instead of using its iconic bossa nova beat), many songs on *The 14th Moon* had pre-existing arrangements. Six of the songs were originally written for other singers, television programs, and commercials before being included on the album.[2] Yuming had covered her compositions before—some of her most well-known songs, such as "Graduation Photograph" (Sotsugyō shashin, 1975), were originally written for other singers—but she had not included so many tracks written for other contexts on her previous albums. These songs testified to her popularity as a songwriter, but they also rendered *The 14th Moon* a "compilation album," in contrast to the unified concept album favored among rock musicians in Japan since the late 1960s.

Sound-wise, *The 14th Moon* formed a natural continuation from Yuming's previous album, *Cobalt Hour*. The keyboards are featured, as in the intros of the first two tracks, "Ripples" and

"The 14th Moon"; the piano plays the rhythmic riff, setting the mood for the whole album. Although Yuming mostly did not play on the album—"Like Nothing Ever Happened" is the only song on which she plays the piano—the emphasis on keyboards smartly retained an image of a piano-playing singer-songwriter. The arrangements on *The 14th Moon* highlight Yuming's fondness for unconventional chord progressions, seventh and ninth chords, and non-chord tones (melody tones that do not belong to the accompanying chord). For example, "Ripples," the opening track of *The 14th Moon*, has seventh and ninth chords that give it a jazzy feel, and the vocal line hovers around the major seventh and ninth of these chords (Ex. 2.1 and 2.2).

Above all, the music serves a larger goal: conveying the lyrics. "Chuo Freeway" creates a vivid image of instability and movement by avoiding the use of a stable key—a fitting musical device for a song about driving on an expressway. "The 14th Moon" concerns a heroine who has made an important decision that makes her heart pound, which is reflected in

Example 2.1 *From the intro of "Ripples" (00:09–00:17).*

Example 2.2 *Two phrases from "Ripples" (00:17–00:20 and 00:26–00:29).*

Example 2.3 *Beginning of "The 14th Moon" (00:00–00:07).*

the upbeat keyboard rhythm of the intro (Ex. 2.3). In both "Where Does Loneliness Go" and "Good Luck and Goodbye," the protagonist unexpectedly encounters her past loved ones. Both songs follow an idiom that recalls mid-twentieth-century jazz standards, thereby communicating nostalgia.

These observations suggest that the variety in musical styles on the album reflects the variety in lyrical themes. But we should not let this observation fool us. Despite Yuming's argument about the lack of "totality" on *The 14th Moon*, the album does carry an overarching theme—one that is so prominent that it permeates virtually every track. Let us take a closer look at its lyrics.

The Beauty of the Moment

A woman is sitting in a car, feeling frustrated for not knowing the feelings of her love interest—the man holding the steering wheel.[3] What will happen, she wonders, when she confesses her love to him? This question makes her heart pound. But instead of feeling anxious, she immerses herself in the feeling of the present moment. It is, after all, a very special point in time, for it carries the promise of infinite possibilities in the future.

This moment is "the fourteenth moon," as experienced in the song of the same name.[4] Like the moon on the fourteenth day of the month, just before it becomes full, it symbolizes a specific liminal space—the threshold preceding fulfillment. As Yuming saw it, the completion ultimately entails a transformation to "emptiness," rendering the moment *before* fulfillment the most desirable state (Arai 1976b, 58). This idea inspired the iconic chorus of "The 14th Moon," an all-time Yuming favorite that she has often sung to close her live performances[5]:

Rather than the full moon, which will wane from the following night,
I love the moon on the fourteenth night the most

"The 14th Moon" encapsulates the recurring themes of the album. First, the song is focused on an individual moment. Yoshida Kaori and essayist Sakai Junko have highlighted that this focus is a distinctive characteristic of Yuming's songs but that these individual moments carry both the weight of the past and the promise of the future (Yoshida 1977, 20; Sakai 2013, 13). As completely as the heroine of "The 14th Moon" immerses herself in the wonderful point of time preceding the "full moon," she still sees that time is inevitably flowing toward an unknown future. In this way, the past and future always converge with the present, which brings forth the darker undertones to which Bourdaghs refers.

The 14th Moon emphasizes this moment-driven aspect by focusing on the protagonists' moods, feelings, thoughts, and impressions instead of presenting a narrative where anything "happens." This approach can be explained by what the popular music scholar David Machin describes as an *activity schema*, that is, "what happens in the song at the most basic level" (Machin 2010, 78–80). Most songs in *The 14th Moon* do not incorporate such a schema—at least one that would be oriented on action and clear goals. Even when such an activity takes place, the focus is rather on introspection aroused by that activity instead of the activity itself. As Machin explains, these kinds of lyrics "are not about acting on the world, but about mental processes and existential states. They are about desires and the moments where we wait for what we desire" (Machin 2010, 96).

Like its title track, *The 14th Moon* embraces the complex emotions that the flow of time inevitably arouses. Examined closer, the flow of time—and the transience it entails—seems almost insidiously intertwined with even the happiest moments. This passage of time can be observed in countless minor details, such as day turning into night in "Chuo Freeway" and "A Summer Place" or summer turning into fall in "Late Summer." It is certainly present in the heroines' encounters with their past loved ones—and the complex emotions caused by the unexpected incursion of the past into the present—in "Where Does Loneliness Go" and "Good Luck and Goodbye." "Like Nothing Ever Happened" remarks that people always come to realize their happiness only after it has become part of their pasts, whereas "The 14th Moon" acknowledges that the precious moment it describes will fade into the past as soon as the heroine enunciates her feelings. Music journalist Hasegawa Makoto has aptly crystallized this aspect of the album:

Since her debut, [Yuming] has been sensitive to the concept of *passing time*. Every passionate love affair will cool off one day. Everything with a form will break down. Every human will die, without exception. Her songs always contain this perspective that coolly faces such realism. (Kirarasha 2003, 32)

But the fundamental stance of Yuming's songs is not lament. While her heroines may admit that their past incorporates an aspect of melancholy, they never focus on regretting mistakes or openly crying over undesired outcomes (Ren'ai kajin kenkyūkai 1996, 170–1). Consider, for example, "Like Nothing Ever Happened," which Yuming wrote as a requiem for her pet dog. For a requiem, the song is conspicuously dispassionate: instead of suggesting mourning, its soothing melody in a major mode and lyrics turn into a more universal, philosophical comment about happiness and memories. But the reassuring atmosphere also masks a lot of melancholy in the lyrics, which are about carrying on while hiding sadness in one's heart:

Chorus: People beautifully carve the things they have lost to their hearts,
So they always, always,
Face tomorrow like nothing ever happened

The subdued atmosphere in "Like Nothing Ever Happened" is in part due to Yuming's singing style. The voice of a singer is often expected to express "the most essential emotions in musical form" (Mayhew 1999, 73), but Yuming's conspicuous lack of vibrato can render her singing almost emotionless. Her blank voice does, however, serve an important role in her work: as Yoshida Kaori has elaborated, it functions like a canvas on which listeners can freely project their interpretations (Yoshida 1977, 17). For example, a voice without vibrato can communicate a lack of emotion—but it can also indicate that the singer is untrained, which may add to her image of sincerity and authenticity.

This is not to say that the music on *The 14th Moon* would be dispassionate. Instead, emotion is expressed by other devices. This is best exemplified by "In the Morning Light," whose heavier sound, musical contrasts, and serious lyrics make it into one of the more dramatic tracks on the album. "In the Morning Light" describes the feelings of its heroine, who has found the love of her life. Instead of feeling happy or fulfilled, however, she is anxious about the future. Her anxiety is not caused by anything concrete nor is it directly related to her loved one. Instead, she is worried about the flow of time and the unpredictability of life:

Making even a rose lose its color,
The flow of time is very frightening

The grand scale of the heroine's emotional world—characterized as a "space" in the bridge—renders her love as an existential state rather than a passing feeling; unlike most of Yuming's protagonists, she steps away from the position of an observer and instead expresses her strong attachment to the present. The music also plays a critical part in conveying this impression. The simple, minor-scale, descending melody of the verse is like a series of melancholic sighs that become a repeating motive, so constant as if to negate the possibility

Example 2.4 *Two examples of sigh-like melodic gestures in "In the Morning Light" (00:25–00:29 and 00:39–00:43).*

of change (Ex. 2.4). The irony is that the music is full of change: with every occurrence of the melody, a new instrument is added, until the music bursts into full instrumentation in the dramatic bridge. While arrangements often add instruments with each repeat of a melody to retain the listener's attention (Hagita 2018, 32–3), in "In the Morning Light" it conveys the heroine's anxiety and enhances the dramatic effect of the lyrics.

The arrangement of "In the Morning Light" also sets it apart from the lighter songs. In particular, the cheerful "Sun Shower" contrasts with "In the Morning Light" by its major mode and fast-paced melody. Whereas the lyrics of "In the Morning Light" are concerned with the transience of time, "Sun Shower" focuses on the moment and makes only little references to the passing of time. Nevertheless, this and other lighter songs also contribute to the album's theme by contrasting with it (which, in effect, underlines its prominence). In addition, they are in the flow of *chronological* time that passes through the whole album: the change of seasons. This can be observed in Table 2.1.

Even with some uncertainties, the pattern seems prominent: the songs constitute a chronology from fall to the end of summer. Explicit references to seasons are typical in Japanese poetry and song lyrics regardless of genre, but *The 14th Moon* engages with seasonal expressions in a significantly

Table 2.1

Seasons in Songs on *The 14th Moon*

Season	Song	Expression of season
Fall	"Ripples"	October
	"The 14th Moon"	Moon (a symbol for fall)
Winter	"Where Does Loneliness Go"	"Calm winter scene"
(no season)	"In the Morning Light"	
(possibly spring)	"Chuo Freeway"	(driving in a convertible or with the window open)
(possibly winter or spring)	"Like Nothing Ever Happened"	"Blizzard of yesterday"
Summer	"Sun Shower"	Sun; surfing
	"A Summer Place"	Summer
(possibly summer)	"Good Luck and Goodbye"	(rain; the rainy season takes place during summer)
From late summer to fall	"Late Summer (The Lonely Season)"	"Late summer"; "cosmos flowers" (a symbol for fall)

more subdued way. Many songs contain only one mention, and they generally avoid obvious seasonal symbols, such as cherry blossoms or Christmas, which are common markers in

Japanese popular music for seasons and the emotions they arouse. For Yuming, the seasons are never the point. Instead, they are contexts coloring the background and assuring that the passing of time is a pervasive theme at both the micro and macro levels of *The 14th Moon*.

Therefore, despite the disparate musical settings of *The 14th Moon*, it is actually based on a unified theme that connects all the tracks to each other and holds the album together. I would argue that the album can thus be considered a concept album and read as a metaphor for the many ways in which time determines and impacts human life. By extension, the heroines' persistent focus on individual moments seems like a temporary escape from this unstoppable flow. In this respect, *The 14th Moon* always incorporates a complex reality within its musical variety.

Cosmopolitan Fantasies

Yuming's sound was constantly described as "cosmopolitan" in the 1970s. She has been characterized as the "storyteller of the metropolis" (Fukami 1989) and recognized as a pioneering figure in incorporating English phrases to Japanese-language songs (Stanlaw 2000). Perhaps because Yuming was associated with contemporary Japanese fashion magazines that projected an internationalized image, many critics have claimed that her music and lyrics are "non-national" (Matsutōya 2011, 32). But Yuming's cosmopolitanness was precisely what impressed the psychologist and feminist writer Ogura Chikako in the 1970s:

[After hearing Yuming's music] I thought that I had finally found a song I wanted to sing myself. Despite being sung in Japanese, it sounded like it was not Japanese. It felt transparent; it was like a European film. (Shimazaki 2006, 86)

On first listening, this cosmopolitanism would also seem to characterize *The 14th Moon*. While "Chuo Freeway" and "Sun Shower" take place in Japan—both refer to locations in Tokyo and Kanagawa—the other songs remain vague about their settings. We can gather that "Where Does Loneliness Go" and "Good Luck and Goodbye" take place in a city; in the latter, the sounds of city traffic are heard during a short interlude. Where this city is located, however, remains ambiguous. We know neither where the drive in "The 14th Moon" takes place nor where the heroines of "In the Morning Light" and "Like Nothing Ever Happened" elaborate on their life. In fact, the songs seem to dispel any clues to exact location deliberately.

Given this vagueness, it seems surprising that *The 14th Moon* was influenced by the shamisen songs (*kouta* and *kiyomoto*) that Yuming practiced in her pre-teen years:

On *The 14th Moon*, there are quite a lot of those kinds of elements. In fact, the title itself is an example. [...] "I like the moon on the fourteenth night, just before it becomes full." Don't you think that's like *kouta*?

I thought, ah, this is good. And so I recalled the *kiyomoto* songs and other things I had studied and made the album. (Matsutōya 1984, 30–1)

This is an association one would certainly not make based on the music. But on closer examination, several details appear to connect the album with various forms of premodern Japanese culture.[6] For example, the season-related words resemble the symbolism in classical *waka* poetry. To those familiar with Yoshida Kenkō's classic, *Essays in Idleness* (Tsurezuregusa, 1330–2), "The 14th Moon" is likely to recall the often-quoted passage about the moon being at its most beautiful when invisible. The impermanence of things (*mujō*), embedded in songs like "In the Morning Light," is a core concept in various schools of Japanese Buddhism and a prominent theme in premodern Japanese literature and poetry. Soon after the release of the album, Yuming also revealed that she deliberately wanted to give it a title in Japanese to distinguish it from the English-language titles of her two previous albums (Arai 1976b, 54).

To be clear, I am not arguing that there is a continuum from premodern Japanese culture to Yuming's album.[7] Rather, I find it curious that Yuming encoded these elements in the songs on *The 14th Moon*, as this "traditional" facet would seem starkly opposed to her cosmopolitan and "non-national" image. Vagueness about place is, of course, not unique to Yuming's music; countless popular songs, including Anglophone ones, avoid referring to specific locations. Apart from rendering an artist cosmopolitan, as in Yuming's case, it can also serve commercial interests by appealing to the broadest audience possible, allowing listeners to relate to the lyrics regardless of where they are located. However, this vagueness can also be deceiving, as songs often embed subtle hints about actual places. To reveal them, David Machin suggests examining *how* the lyrics are articulated instead of only addressing *what* they say (Machin 2010, 92–4). By following this approach, one notices that several aspects of *The 14th Moon* locate the songs in specifically Japanese, even "traditional" contexts. In the implementation of these techniques, the use of the Japanese language incorporates a central role.

Consider "Late Summer," which refers to the heroine's *furusato* ("hometown"). A concept associated with one's roots in the countryside, it is constantly used in *enka*, a Japanese-style popular song genre (Yano 2002, 168–9). "Late Summer" describes the change of seasons and times of day through the transforming colors of the sky:

Chorus: Indigo blue [*aiiro*] turns to ultramarine [*gunjō*]
Twilight [*hakubo*] turns to purple [*murasaki*]

These lyrics draw on premodern Japanese culture in two ways. First, the words for different colors are shades used in traditional fabrics and painting.[8] Many of them would typically not be used in everyday speech because of their poetic connotations, but Yuming would have been familiar with them, as the child of a kimono fabric shop owner and as an art student who majored in *Nihonga* (Japanese-style painting). In the 1970s, Yuming's melodies and lyrics were often compared to painting and the visual arts (Shūkan heibon 1976, 44). But whereas the comparison was typically made with (Western) watercolor painting, the colors of "Late Summer" seem to "paint" the lyrics in the style of *Nihonga*. This may be a device for communicating a return to the old; in the lyrics, the heroine comes back to her concrete and symbolic *furusato*, which remains largely unchanged despite changes in her life.

Second, portraying one's feelings through the change of seasons is a common device in classical *waka* poetry, where fall often symbolizes the de-intensification of romantic feelings (Raud 1994, 44). Apart from the chorus of "Late Summer," Yuming also applies the device in individual wordings. In the two fall songs that suggest the end of a romance, "Late Summer" and "Ripples," Yuming uses the word "fall" (*aki*). In *waka*, the word often denotes the waning of romantic feelings, as it is homophonic with "satiation" (Raud 1994, 44).

A similar device is applied in "A Summer Place." The Caribbean calypso-like style and references to Campari suggest that the song takes place in an international holiday resort. This resort may well be at a seaside town in Japan, but the music and lyrics, punctuated by the English phrase, "You are my sunshine," evoke images of the West. However, an interesting rupture to these images is brought about by Japanese culture-specific expressions, such as *komorebi* (sunlight filtering through trees) and *takezaiku* (bamboo work). These expressions not only call out the heroine's Japaneseness but also re-localize the song in a Japanese context: it resembles the idealized images of holiday resorts that one constantly encountered in Japanese commercial magazines at that time (Gluck 1993, 75).

Another type of device concerns the presentation of lyrics in visual form. One of the distinctive features of the literary cultures of logogram-based written languages (such as Chinese and Japanese) is that they often construct meaning on visual instead of aural perception. For example, if one is only familiar with the grammar and the meanings of the characters, it is possible to read classical Chinese poetry without any knowledge of Chinese pronunciation. The priority of visual presentation concerns much of Japanese poetry as well. While song lyrics cannot be entirely equated with written poetry—they fulfill their meaning only when performed as songs—Japanese-language lyrics often engage with these visual attributes. For example, lyricists may assign unconventional readings to the words they use or take advantage of the enormous amount of homophones in the Japanese language (Yamada 2014, 142–5).[9] These devices result in intriguing double meanings that cannot be fathomed based only on aural perception.

"The 14th Moon" engages with a similar technique, but in a highly peculiar way. The lyrics contain two Japanese-language proverbs, *iwanu ga hana* (silence is golden) and *yanagi ni kaze* (no reply is best).[10] Both are old sayings that trace back to the Edo period (1603–1868) or earlier; as such, they seem out of place in Yuming's "city" world. Yet in "The 14th Moon," they are rendered more cosmopolitan by the use of the Roman alphabet. A similar interplay of languages concerns the filler, "um...," that accompanies them. While written in English, it could also be read in Japanese as *umu*, an expression that roughly translates as "uh huh" or "hmm." This mix of languages and writing systems also concerns the cover of the album, where everything—including Japanese-language song titles—is written in the Roman alphabet. A practice that Yuming adopted also on her earlier albums, it aestheticizes the familiar by rendering it anew, resulting in a process of re-exotification that renders Japan and the Japanese language as parts of Yuming's cosmopolitan image. Therefore, the mix of writing systems is not entirely analogous with the "non-national" imagery encountered in much of contemporary visual media, such as fashion magazines (Shigematsu 2005). Instead, it represents a brand of cosmopolitanism that contextualizes in a markedly Japanese setting.

It is intriguing how conspicuously these expressions of place differed from the images generally associated with Yuming's work. For example, her previous albums included such songs as "Velvet Easter" (1973) and "Oh My Françoise" (Watashi no Furansowāzu, 1974), which connected her music with images of Western culture. So does the general sound of *The 14th Moon*, to be sure, but it also presents Japan as a site onto which these cosmopolitan fantasies could be projected. This interplay of different cultural images certainly contributed to Yuming's "distant yet attainable" image by synthesizing familiar and excitingly fresh elements with each other. Apart from the lyrics, however, the album also expresses a similar interplay in the music. To demonstrate this, let us examine the song that is continuously ranked as a critics' and fans' favorite among Yuming's work: "Chuo Freeway."

Riding the Chuo Freeway

A car is sweeping the Chūō Expressway in Tokyo, carrying a young couple. The woman is sitting on the front seat, her boyfriend holding the steering wheel with one hand and her shoulder with another. It is gradually getting darker, the sunset already coloring the front glass yellow. The woman observes a passing racetrack on the right and a beer factory on the left: her home is approaching.[11] This makes the drive a precious moment, for it represents a liminal space between being together and separation.

Indeed, a more melancholic side shadows this wonderful drive. Because of the strong wind—apparently, the couple is driving in a convertible or with the windows open—the man would not even hear it if the woman said, "I love you." Nevertheless, she is not feeling down; instead, she simply hopes that this moment—her being close to him—would never end. And this is when something magical happens. The "twinkling city lights" around the car seem like stars, and the car itself becomes a shooting star that journeys among them. What seemed like an ordinary drive home turns into a wondrous alternative reality, with the mundane expressway suddenly looking like a runway going all the way to the sky. It is as if time has stopped, with only the car and the couple existing in the whole universe.

Like so many songs on *The 14th Moon*, "Chuo Freeway" vividly captures the diverse, contradictory emotions packed in an individual moment that cannot escape the flow of time. With subtle use of words, it transforms an ordinary drive into a magical experience, projecting its heroine's subjective emotions to her surroundings. Also the title subtly participates in interweaving fantasy and reality by rendering the mundane Chūō Expressway (*Chūō jidōshadō*) a more exciting and cosmopolitan "Chuo Freeway" (*Chūō furīwei*).

Yuming originally wrote "Chuo Freeway" for the *Seven Star Show*, which the television network TBS ran from February to March 1976. Each episode featured a well-known singer, ranging from enka and pop stars such as Mori Shin'ichi and Sawada Kenji to folk singer-songwriters such as Yoshida Takurō. Yuming—the only female artist featured in the show—made a joint appearance with rock musician Kamayatsu Hiroshi. The two had known each other since the days when the teenage Yuming was hanging out with rock musicians, and

Kamayatsu produced her debut single in 1972—although he later confessed that his laissez-faire approach was not an ideal match with Yuming's perfectionism (Matsuki 2016, 127). Nevertheless, in the *Seven Star Show*, these two different musicians were asked to write a song for each other. Yuming's song for Kamayatsu was "Chuo Freeway."

Along with "Sun Shower," "Chuo Freeway" is the only song on *The 14th Moon* that refers to specific locations in Japan. A relatively uncommon practice in Yuming's songs at that time, this aspect spurred literary scholar Uchida Tatsuru to argue that the song's depiction of locations in Tokyo is analogous to the concept of *kunihome* (the celebration of national locations) in classical Chinese and Japanese poetry (Shaku et al. 2010, 50–1). Regardless of whether one agrees with Uchida's argument or not, it does demonstrate that Yuming's approach of depicting Japan from the viewpoint of cosmopolitan youth culture was considered extraordinary.

However, it is not only the lyrics that create the effect of a magical moment. As Fukami Haruka has described, the feeling of a drive arises from a vivid interplay between the lyrics and the music:

> After the intro, the song begins to slide away from a stable tonality, emphasizing a floating feeling […]. The feeling of speed, the feeling of one's body floating in the air, the feeling of one's hair flowing in the wind, and the feeling of movement […] are created with the help of the skillful arrangement. (Fukami 1989, 30)

What Fukami describes can be observed at the beginning of the song (Ex. 2.5). The effect of motion is achieved through

Example 2.5 *Opening melody and chords of "Chuo Freeway" (00:09–00:21).*

frequent tonicizations (temporary arrivals on a new key) that occur in every other measure; aside from two intervening diminished chords, they outline the sequence F-D-Gm-C-Fm-B♭-E♭-A♭. Matsutōya Masataka, who watched Yuming write the song, later revealed that he was worried whether she would be able to complete the song without getting entangled in a never-ending series of tonicizations (Matsutōya 2016, 77). However, the harmonic complexity serves an important function by interplaying with the lyrics: it resounds with the image of a car, shifting from lane to lane as it speeds down the expressway. The constant rotations of chords create a feeling of instability and movement.

The bridge, by contrast, is harmonically stable and only alternates between two chords (D♭maj⁷–A♭maj⁷). The modulation to a new key, A♭ major, creates a new tonal space that contrasts with the verse, combined with a melody sung at higher pitch. This musical change aptly colors the lyrics, which shift focus away from the actual surroundings to the heroine's imagination:

The city lights begin to twinkle
It's as if the two of us have become a shooting star

With this device, the music enhances the duality of the lyrics: it creates a contrast between the drive on the expressway (movement) and the world of imagination (stability). In the end, it is this magical, imaginary level that remains. After the final line that compares the freeway to a runway to the night sky is repeated three times, the listener would anticipate the music to conclude on the tonic, A♭. Instead, the song ends on a G♭m⁹ chord, which remains unresolved. The music gradually fades away in this new tonal space—the night sky—with the instruments vibrantly conveying the image of a continuing imaginative drive among the stars.

"Chuo Freeway" paints this magical moment in such a vibrant way that it is no wonder the song has kept on captivating the hearts of the audience, even forty years after the release of *The 14th Moon*. The fantastic elements are interesting, however, because the song is based on Yuming's life. Matsutōya Masataka often drove her home from central Tokyo to Hachiōji on the Chūō Expressway before the two got married (Matsutōya 1984, 125) and proposed to her on one of these drives (Matsutōya 2011, 18). To what extent, then, is *The 14th Moon* autobiographical?

Fictional Worlds, Lived Experiences

Yuming was often asked whether her songs stemmed from personal experiences. Unlike many other Japanese singer-songwriters, she categorically denied any confessionalism in her music in the 1970s (Ren'ai kajin kenkyūkai 1996, 111). This seems odd, considering that many songs on *The 14th Moon* have parallels with her life. "Chuo Freeway" is an obvious example. Another one would be "Like Nothing Ever Happened," a requiem for her dog. And, considering that Yuming was getting married soon after the release of the album, "In the Morning Light" may well depict the anxiety the heroine experiences before her wedding.[12]

However, Yuming had a different explanation: instead of writing songs about her own life, she wished to transform her lived experiences into different types of atmospheres (Kitanaka 1979, 42). Thus, what Yuming sings on *The 14th Moon* may be fiction but renders her real-life experiences into imaginary worlds. I believe that this observation explains *The 14th Moon*'s dream-like aura. By constantly integrating wondrous elements into everyday experiences, the album draws the listener to a musical space of intriguing contrasts and interweaves the familiar with the new through various musical, lyrical, and visual devices. Subtly signaling time and place, the songs immerse the listener and construct Yuming's "distant yet attainable" image.

But how distant or attainable was Yuming to contemporary listeners? Because Yuming mixes lived experiences with fiction, her songs are assumed to say much about the world in which they were created. We will next see that this observation adds yet another fascinating aspect of transformation to *The 14th Moon*.

3 New Music

Some people say that my lyrics don't have a feeling of real life, but I don't think that only gloomy and dark songs constitute a feeling of real life. Having a croissant and café au lait after waking up in the morning is the life of young women today, so I think that's today's feeling of real life.

– YUMING (HIGASHI 1981, 51)

Reading Tanaka Yasuo's novel, *Somehow, Crystal* (Nantonaku, kurisutaru, 1980) can at first seem like a confusing experience. Published amidst a growing consumerist boom in Japan, the literary bestseller and recipient of the prestigious Bungei Prize focuses on a young woman in Tokyo who builds her identity on consumption. Living the "crystal" lifestyle, as the novel refers to it, centers on consuming posh youth brands, listening to fashionable music, eating at fancy restaurants and cafes, and indulging in romance with other boys and girls who enjoy the crystal life.

Much more noted than the main story, however, is the novel's infamous 442 endnotes that explain the countless brand names and buzzwords mentioned by the protagonist (Smith 2020). Considering that the endnotes focus on brands (almost all of which are Western), the one dedicated to Yuming sticks out. The note itself is essentially nonsense; the annotator is imagining Yuming's posh apartment in the style of housing advertisements (Tanaka 1981, 170). More interestingly, Tanaka's listing Yuming as a "brand" echoed her public image: in contemporary Japan, Yuming's music was largely regarded as a symbol of the affluent, urban lifestyle that Tanaka portrayed in his book. With Yuming herself having called her sound "middle-class," "leisure-class," even "bourgeois," the press once characterized her as "the most *crystal* woman" (Shūkan yomiuri 1981, 164).[1]

But as consumption-oriented as the crystal world was, Yuming's music was not regarded as a mere consumable; it carried an image of artistic depth and sophistication. Although Yuming consciously molded herself for the commercial market, she avoided accusations of having "sold out" (Bourdaghs 2012, 183–4). How does commercialism manifest itself on *The 14th Moon*—or does it? How does the album connect with the broader context of contemporary Japanese popular music and society? The story begins with a fundamental aspect of music: genre.

The Emancipation of Commercialism

When Alfa Music was about to release *Vapor Trail*, Murai Kunihiko went to discuss the album with the marketing department at Toshiba EMI. Convinced that Yuming would become a leading figure in introducing a more "international" sound to Japanese music, Murai felt confident about marketing her songs. His confidence, however, was soon countered by an issue that he would face countless times thereafter: Yuming's music did not fit into any pre-existing genres (Matsuki 2016, 148).

This comment might be understandable if it concerned *The 14th Moon*, which is so stylistically diverse. For Yuming's earlier albums, however, it seems more puzzling. Even with cross-generic elements, their characteristic pop-rock sound would fit neatly into, say, adult-oriented rock or soft rock. But these Anglo-American genre classifications did not exist in contemporary Japanese popular music, and executives were confused by the perceived similarity of Yuming's songs with Western music. As music producer Shimokōbe Seizō explained:

> When I listened to [Yuming's album], I thought it was Western music made by a Japanese musician. It was sung in Japanese, but the feeling was Western. Of course the Japanese music department would get confused with this kind of stuff. (Matsuki 2016, 158)

In other words, Yuming's musical style placed her in a liminal zone. Although Murai and Shimokōbe admired her "international" flavor, she had to be classified according to genres established for Japanese musicians. Murai became worried: since genre helps to locate the artist within the market, it needs to be legible to both industry and audience (Holt 2007). Bluntly put, an artist without a recognizable genre is at the risk of falling between the cracks.

The issue with Yuming's music was that it combined elements from seemingly opposite production models: the commercial mainstream music industry (*kayōkyoku*) and musician-led production that claimed a more authentic and arguably less commercial alternative to the mainstream (genres such as rock and folk). In practice, the division between the two was never as strict as public discourse claimed, but the perceived differences help to explain why Yuming's music was originally met with such bewilderment.[2]

Kayōkyoku was produced as commercial entertainment for audiences of all ages and virtually always remained neutral on social issues (although this "neutrality" is contestable, as explained later). The roles of performer, lyricist, composer, and producer were separated, and artist management and producers oversaw the public image of singers. Musically diverse, kayōkyoku incorporated genres such as enka and idol (*aidoru*) pop. Television was a significant medium for disseminating kayōkyoku, and various ranking programs such as *This Night's Hit Studio* and *The Best Ten* made the songs a ubiquitous presence in Japanese television in the 1970s and 1980s (Nagahara 2017, 212–15). And as television was so influential in everyday life, kayōkyoku songs and performers were omnipresent in everyday culture (Zettsu 2002, 8–9; Hase & Ōta 2007).

By contrast, folk singer-songwriters and rock musicians were careful not to be identified as "mere performers" working for commercial profit. They tended to emphasize their musicianship and artistic integrity by writing and producing their own material, occasionally introducing rebellious lyrics. Since their approach was incompatible with the commercial aspirations and production model of kayōkyoku, these musicians began to establish their own record companies in the late 1960s. Companies such as URC and Elec allowed musicians to produce original works that they could disseminate themselves and subvert the sociopolitical order through recorded music. To distance themselves further from kayōkyoku, they mostly avoided performances on television. Although social commentary became far less prominent in the early 1970s, rock and folk nevertheless emitted an aura of authenticity, in part supported by the discourse about their claimed disinterest in commercial matters.[3]

In such an environment, Yuming represented a bizarre combination. She was a singer-songwriter, but she detested folk; she emphasized her artistic integrity but openly embraced commercialism; she was a Japanese musician, but her sound was perceived to be closer to Western music. In other words, her approach took in aspects of rock, folk, and kayōkyoku—but it was not dedicated to any single mold. Yuming herself recognized this ambivalence by drawing a line between her music and folk:

> The reason why my songs became popular is that the style
> of folk was so crude, with many songs having […] a sense
> of poverty. My songs were entirely different from that; they
> were classy and carried a rich feeling full of dreams. I think this
> matches the current era well. (Shūkan heibon 1976, 44)

Unsurprisingly, Yuming's disdain of folk outraged fans of that genre.[4] However, while suggesting that these other genres had become outdated, her comment also implies that her popularity was indicative of a broader social shift.

Japan was indeed undergoing a notable transformation around the time of Yuming's debut. The seemingly unstoppable economic growth of the 1960s, paired with rapid urbanization, had turned the country into a global economic superpower.[5] Following the antiwar and other movements that spurred politically oriented folk in the 1960s, the 1970s gradually saw a cooling of rebelliousness, to be replaced by the rise of a consumerist boom that centered in big cities like Tokyo and Osaka. With more than 90 percent of the population identifying as "middle class" in the early 1970s, much of Japanese society saw itself as a uniform nation with the same shared values (Tsurumi 1984, 108–38). This conception became broadly popularized and was reflected in contemporary media and popular culture (Gluck 1993, 75–6; Nagahara 2017, 210–11).[6] For example, whereas leftist and anti-US movements had a strong foothold among youth in the 1960s, the generation that came of age in the 1970s embraced consumerism as a virtue and was much more receptive to influence from the United States. The phenomenon was manifested in the conspicuous consumption forwarded in fashion magazines such as *City Road* and *Popeye*, which shunned political themes and instead burst with cosmopolitan images of an affluent and idealized America (Komori 2011).

Therefore, when the music journalist Yazawa Kan argued that Yuming turned "muddy and sloppy" folk songs into "sophisticated and fashionable" city music, he encapsulated the social shift that Yuming's work symbolized (Yazawa 1991, 125). While her songs were originally met with bewilderment in the music industry, her assimilation of urbanization, commercialization, apoliticism, and authorship soon became the soundtrack of the generation that Tanaka Yasuo portrayed in *Somehow, Crystal*. This soundtrack was classified as a genre in the mid-1970s, coined New Music (*nyū myūjikku*).[7]

Yuming had such an indispensable role in defining the discourse about New Music that virtually all contemporary and subsequent accounts recognize her as an archetypal

New Music singer-songwriter.[8] She often took pride in this recognition; after all, it confirmed the popular conception that she had instigated something "new":

> [A]s for New Music—though I dislike the term—well, I created that kind of music. After all, I started from zero. So, my music can't be compared to anything done in the past. (Matsutōya 1984, 9)

Yuming's music was, of course, continuously compared to everything done in the past, for one surely cannot understand "new" without knowing the "old." Although contemporary commentators noted the novelty of her approaches, the development toward combining commercialism with musicianship had in fact begun with earlier rock and folk musicians. Rock group Happy End merged poetic lyrics portraying city life with commercial aspirations in the early 1970s, and this development intensified with many folk singer-songwriters. Yoshida Takurō was noted for starting "New Folk," which turned the dour image of the genre into optimistic youth music that triumphed commercially (Take 1999, 138–40). Whereas iconic sociopolitical folk songs of the 1960s, such as Okabayashi Nobuhiko's "San'ya Blues" (1968) and Nakagawa Gorō's "Examination Blues" (Jukensei burūsu, 1968), highlighted societal pressures concerning blue-collar workers and students, Yoshida's smash hit "Let's Get Married" (Kekkon shiyō yo, 1971) helped to change the image of folk with its portrayal of romance.

As these comparisons exemplify, genre boundaries are not absolute. "New Music" was also a marketing concept, or a "label that record companies conveniently put on the music," as described by Yamamoto Takashi, the editor-in-chief of the *Young Guitar* magazine (Shūkan heibon 1978, 47). In fact, before the invention of the term "New Music" around the mid-1970s, Yuming was often positioned in a longer continuum of folk singer-songwriters. She was even characterized as a "female Takurō" in the early stages of her career (Matsutōya 1984, 10).

However, this characterization misses the novelty of her musical style and sound compared with folk musicians. Although Yoshida and many other folk singer-songwriters were classified under New Music in the mid-1970s, they typically still followed the distinct characteristics of folk by accompanying themselves with an acoustic guitar and by drawing on folk and country from the United States. In contrast, early New Music artists like Yuming, Nakajima Miyuki, Kisugi Takao, and Kaze were from the beginning open to experimenting with a wider array of styles such as pop, adult-oriented rock, funk, jazz, bossa nova, samba, soul, and R&B (Kuji 1982, 35). An attempt to bring down stylistic boundaries was often recognized as a distinct characteristic of the genre (Aono 1976, 123). Because of the perceived novelty of this approach, Yoshida credited Yuming for having created "a field that was entirely different" from the music by folk singer-songwriters (Take 1999, 172).

Apart from stylistic diversity, the "newness" of New Music was recognized in its polished sound and richer instrumentation, emphasis on introspection and nostalgia, apolitical lyrics, and the performers' flashy images.[9] Commercialization and introspective lyrics had already become common in the work of folk artists like Yoshida Takurō and Kaguyahime, but whereas their music at least hinted at social commentary (albeit in a commercially attractive form), the discourse on New Music defined it as an "apolitical" genre from the beginning (Take 1999, 138–40).

While typically discussed as a change within the music industry, these musical and performative distinctions in fact reflected the social conditions of an increasingly consumerist society. Consider the implications of the typical instrumentation. In the DIY ethos of folk, the guitar symbolized egalitarianism, as virtually anyone could grab the instrument to accompany their singing (Azami 2004, 169). By contrast, the piano played by many New Music singer-songwriters not only required musical training but also signified prestige and sophistication in twentieth-century Japan (Tokita 2010). Both the lyrics and elaborate sound subtly communicated images of individualism and affluence that triumphed among city youth in the 1970s.

The public enthusiastically embraced this change. Gradually supplanting earlier styles of folk and kayōkyoku, New Music became the most commercially successful popular music genre in the latter half of the 1970s. Its popularity did not go unnoticed by the kayōkyoku industry, either, which began to hire New Music artists as professional songwriters. They were much more incentivized to collaborate with the kayōkyoku industry than many rock and folk musicians in the 1960s had been; openly commercialist aspirations no longer formed an obstacle for artistic ambitions. However, an important point still distinguished New Music from consumable brands and kayōkyoku in contemporary discourse. It was the genre's positioning as "art."

Artistic Authenticities

A "singer-songwriter" is much more than a musician who performs her own material. She is the ultimate author in charge of her musicianship—a poet-composer devoted to expressing her innermost thoughts in an individual manner. A symbol of artistic integrity, she commands cultural relevance beyond her role as a musician and as an individual author (Bentley 2018).

It sometimes seems amazing how culturally specific concepts can be naturalized from one country to another. The authenticity associated with singer-songwriters in Japan in the 1970s is a fascinating example: although New Music grew out of specific developments in Japan, the Japanese discourses surrounding singer-songwriters paralleled the ideals that were associated with their foreign contemporaries like Leonard Cohen, Bob Dylan, and Joni Mitchell. Although popular songs typically emerge from collaboration, the discourse in Japan centered on the singer-songwriters' individual creativity, establishing them as uncompromised *authors*. This status was used to justify the commercialism of New Music and to draw a distinction from kayōkyoku: according to the popular image, singer-songwriters had not succumbed to commercial forces but harnessed the industry to assert their individual vision (Stevens 2008, 47–8). As a Japanese management company representative summarized, "When kayōkyoku tops the charts, it's thanks to the production organization, but in New Music it's all about the musician, including everything from the artist's sound and lyrics to philosophical aspects" (Shūkan heibon 1981, 145).

This image of individual creativity was reflected in New Music production. The influential record company For Life Records, for example, was founded in 1975 to bestow all authorship to musicians; as such, it was celebrated for its production model that freed creative musicians from the constraints of the commercial industry (Tomisawa 1979, 203–9). Less emphasis was given to the fact that the company was also successful business-wise and that its founders, including Yoshida Takurō and Inoue Yōsui, collaborated with the kayōkyoku industry as songwriters (Shūkan heibon 1978, 50). Singer-songwriters were also keen to assert their individual creativity: arranger Hagita Mitsuo later described his bewilderment at singer-songwriters who insisted on holding onto their artistic vision when he tried to make their music more commercially attractive (Hagita 2018, 46). Another similar example is singer-songwriters' practice of releasing their music only when "it felt complete" instead of releasing a new album when it was bound to succeed commercially (Shūkan heibon 1978, 51). For example, when *The 14th Moon* was released, more than a year had passed since *Cobalt Hour*—a hiatus too long to imagine for a kayōkyoku singer at the height of her popularity.[10]

Yet the rise of New Music to a commercially successful genre could have posed a risk to its image of authenticity, not least because commercialism in popular music has always been criticized as a sign of its lesser artistic value. Yuming's strategy to overcome this issue was to consciously construct her image as a serious artist. To begin with, she emphasized her musicianship by distinguishing between money-making aspirations and artistic ambitions. Throughout the 1970s, she underlined that she made music not "for the money" but "as a hobby."[11] Strongly echoing the Romantic notion that the true artist was more interested in self-expression than worldly matters, this statement also resonated with the ideals of singer-songwriters in Europe and America (Bentley 2018). Furthermore, the cover of *Vapor Trail* was modeled after the classical record label Archiv Musik's iconic layout (Arai 1976b, 54), and Alfa Music advertised Yuming's debut as the emergence of a musical neo-sensualist school (*shin kankaku-ha*)—a reference to a Japanese literary trend represented by novelists such as the Nobel Prize-winner Kawabata Yasunari.

This strategy was highly successful. According to the influential music journalist Tomisawa Issei, musicians like Yuming gradually occupied the public sphere that had previously been reserved for novelists. Echoing a popular view in the contemporary discussion, Tomisawa declared that Yuming was not a "celebrity" but an "artist" (Tomisawa 1976, 88). His arguments coincided with a general acceptance of popular songs as "legitimate"culture among intellectuals (Nagahara 2017, 214–20), which further enabled new kinds of artist identities for singer-songwriters. Yuming's background in classical music and interest in literature, for example, gave her work an aura of sophistication and depth. The composer and popular essayist Dan Ikuma even placed her work alongside the modern tradition of Japanese vocal music by classical composers: "When I heard [Yuming's songs], I was extremely surprised and deeply impressed, because they were a leap above older, overly sentimental songs—a leap that Japanese composers had previously tried to achieve but were not able to" (Dan 1977, 4).

Yuming's skillful creation of her image between art and entertainment was also exemplified by her relationship with the mass media in the 1970s. By the time Yuming made her debut, it had become an established practice that singer-songwriters would not appear on television if they wanted to retain their image of artistic authenticity. Therefore, while Yuming gladly gave interviews to celebrity and fashion magazines, she almost categorically turned down invitations to appear on television, instead focusing on live and radio performances. The decision not to appear on television concerned not only the immensely popular weekly kayōkyoku shows but also the New Year's music spectacle *Kōhaku utagassen* (Red and White Song Contest). In contemporary Japan, this practice was largely seen as a sign of her commitment to "music itself" (Ugaya 2005, 70–1)—a notion that Yuming herself often implied. When explaining why she did not perform in music shows, she emphasized her role as a creative author invested in releasing longer musical works (albums) instead of small-scale commodities (singles):

> I hate being tied up for hours only to sing one song. I think of myself as a songwriter, so I would rather spend that time writing music. Besides, it would be risky for me to sing only one song, because the songs I release as singles only express the exaggerated aspects of my style. (Suzuki 1976, 57)

What Yuming implicitly criticized was the catalogue-like quality of kayōkyoku shows, in which each singer was usually expected to perform their newest single. Weekly music shows were an important and extremely popular genre of television programming, but while presented as "objective rankings," they effectively functioned as advertisement for the music industry (Ogawa 1988, 112–13). This is precisely the kind of commodification that New Music singer-songwriters shunned in the mid-1970s.

However, popular music and television had become increasingly enmeshed since the mid-1960s, and television was such an important venue for determining common trends that it was exceedingly risky for an entertainer not to appear on television at all (Tsurumi 1984, 121–3). To overcome this issue, Yuming adopted a dissemination strategy that had been started by Yoshida Takurō and combined the most desirable attributes of kayōkyoku and New Music: while Yuming tended not to perform on television herself, she gladly wrote songs for dramas, commercials, and kayōkyoku singers.[12] By this approach, she managed to secure a ubiquitous presence for her songs while retaining her image as an uncompromised author.[13]

We already saw how this strategy helped to raise Yuming to nationwide popularity with "Those Were the Days," but *The 14th Moon* is also a perfect example of this strategy. Of the ten songs on the album, four were written for television programs or commercials and two for other singers, who then popularized the songs in kayōkyoku shows. This strategy blurred the line between advertising and performance. For example, while Yuming wrote "A Summer Place" for a summer campaign for Isetan department store and "Good Luck and Goodbye" for Okazaki Yuki, both also effectively advertised *The 14th Moon*. Yuming's music was thus integrated into commercial media and subliminally advertised in countless different contexts, even if the artist herself stayed away from the televised spotlight.

Therefore, although it was commonly argued in the 1970s that Yuming "does not perform on television" or that she made music "only for self-expression," these views should be above all understood as the result of skillful construction of her public image. This construction also highlights another important aspect of New Music: one's authorship pertained not only to her songs but also to her image.

The 14th Moon and Its Social Contexts

The observations above explain much about how *The 14th Moon* is structured. Its stylistic variety, emphasis on keyboards, and introspective lyrics are archetypal characteristics of New Music, but these attributes also communicate a larger theme: the social change that Japan was undergoing at the time of the album's release. In this respect, the album, with its sound and compilation-like quality, not only represents the perfect soundtrack for the "crystal" generation but also serves as a musical window to the Japanese society at that time.

As positively as the notions of authenticity and authorship were perceived in New Music, however, they are shadowed by a long discriminatory legacy. The Romantic notions of authorship are not mere neutral evaluations celebrating individual creativity but have historically been considered exclusively male characteristics (Mayhew 1999). While this observation pertains to Europe and the United States, discourses about popular music and creativity in modern Japan have largely adopted the gender based evaluations that have originated in Western music (Kitagawa 1999, 203–5; Minamida et al. 2019, 70–1). Despite her popularity and wide public recognition, even Yuming was not exempt from being evaluated with certain gender-based stereotypes. To better understand her position and the significance of *The 14th Moon* for her career, we shift our attention to women's roles in contemporary Japan.

4 Women's Images

I think there are two types of men: those that see women as women, and those that see women as human beings. To me, it's imperative that I'm seen as a human being.
– YUMING (SEVENTEEN 1981, 53)

The rumors started circulating a few months before the release of *The 14th Moon*. Yuming, despite her immense popularity, would retire after the release of her upcoming album.

Needless to say, fans were shocked. *Shūkan heibon*, a magazine about public entertainment for young women, lamented the gap that Yuming's retirement would inevitably leave in Japanese popular music:

> [Yuming's retirement] will certainly have a great impact on
> the world of New Music and on female singer-songwriters
> who have started to emerge after her debut. Above all, it
> is a pity for fans who will not be able to enjoy the unique
> showmanship of her performances anymore. (Shūkan heibon
> 1976, 42–3)

The curious thing about these rumors is that virtually nothing supported them. Yuming never suggested that she would end her career after *The 14th Moon*, nor did anyone with whom she worked. She had temporarily reduced her workload in 1976, but considering all that she was going through, this should not have surprised anyone. When finally asked about her plans to retire, Yuming angrily denied the claims (Shūkan heibon 1976; Shūkan myōjō 1976a). Her fans were relieved—but no one still questioned the way her early retirement was proclaimed with such certainty.

The rumors emerged for a simple reason: Yuming and Matsutōya Masataka had gotten engaged in December 1975. But why did their engagement instigate these rumors? Why were they repeated with such certainty?

The Archetypical Housewife

In 1962, Teruoka Yasutaka, a professor of Japanese literature at Waseda University, became irritated with the growing number of female students. Teruoka saw no point in educating women; after all, he reasoned, most of them were bound to become housewives anyway. Teruoka was particularly worried that these women, who, he claimed, had turned Japanese universities into "bridal schools," were unfairly taking places that should have gone to male students (Teruoka 1962). After Teruoka voiced his opinion in several essays and interviews, his assertions instigated a long debate. It was soon coined into an infamous buzzword: "coeds ruining the nation."[1]

Teruoka's views attracted harsh counterarguments. Since gender equality had been officially recognized in the postwar constitution, many were angered by his views and stood up to defend women's right to education. However, Teruoka also gained wide support. After all, he was simply voicing the thoughts of many others.

At the time Teruoka came out with his views, Japan had just entered a period of high economic growth. This growth was largely credited to industrial complexes and their "corporate warriors" (*kigyō senshi*)—the dutiful white-collar male workers, who were willing to sacrifice all their time to their employers, in exchange for economic security for their families. The narrative about their sacrifices, however, neglects the fact that postwar growth from the 1950s to the 1970s was significantly supported by the nuclearization of the family, which was a by-product of the rapid urbanization discussed in the previous chapter (Ueno 2009). The urban nuclear family brought about a middle-class ideal based on a binary segregation of gender roles in public discussion: while men were encouraged to work outside the home as breadwinners, women were expected to devote themselves to being homemakers. These expectations divided women and men between *private* (domestic) and *public* (education, business, politics) spheres, echoing trends in Western Europe and North America at the time. As Andrew Gordon describes: "A society where women of all social strata managed the home, while their men managed the workplace, came to be understood as the natural way things were and ought to be" (Gordon 2005, 425).

In reality, the situation was more complex. An increasing number of middle-class women enrolled in universities and found employment after graduation. While the social norms of the time encouraged those working to leave their jobs at marriage or, at the latest, upon becoming pregnant, many women continued to work after having children (Shiota 2000). But the 1960s did mark a decrease in the percentage of women participating in the labor force, while the percentage of housewives kept increasing.[2] By the early 1980s, most married women worked as professional housewives (Ministry of Health, Labour and Welfare 2015, 1).

The binary gender-based division of labor was supported by the state and the media, and it was generally accepted that this way of organizing families would serve the national project of growing the economy: Japanese discourse in the 1970s heralded the housewife as an indispensable contributor to society (Gordon 2005). Many housewives also enjoyed a high level of agency within their homes, overseeing all matters in the domestic sphere. However, the expectations embedded in the role also restricted many women's lives. The labor market effectively encouraged married women to become economically dependent on men by denying them opportunities for serious advancement or discouraging them from returning to work after childbirth; this was especially the case at large companies (Ueno 2009). To be sure, married men were equally dependent on their wives, without whose domestic labor their professional dedication would have been impossible (Edwards 2014). However, within this structure, many married women's economic dependence on their husbands restricted their broader social agency (Shiota 2000).

Although not all women were housewives, women's images in the mid-1970s were so defined by the ideal of the domestic sphere that the "state of being a housewife [...] was practically synonymous with womanhood" (Ochiai 1996, 35). The media incorporated a significant role in constructing a "chain of equivalence between woman = wife = mother" by actively promoting the notion that women could attain true happiness only by devoting themselves to family life (Shigematsu 2005,

567; Ueno 2012). This concept was eventually accepted by the majority of the Japanese: according to a survey conducted in 1979, 70.1 percent of women and 76.6 percent of men agreed that women should ideally focus on housework while men should work outside the home (Gender Equality Bureau Cabinet Office 2021, 111). How was this status quo reflected in popular music?

Women in Popular Music

When Yuming's engagement to Matsutōya Masataka was revealed, reactions were mixed. Yuming's fans were happy for her, but many became worried about the future of her career. One article in *Shūkan myōjō*, a celebrity magazine for young women, openly lamented how Yuming's marriage would change her career: "A full-scale Yuming boom has finally started, so it's a pity that she is getting married this fall" (Shūkan myōjō 1976a, 49). Such comments show how the popular music industry reinforced women's roles in postwar Japan: even highly popular female musicians were expected to quit professional life when they marry.

For example, When Misora Hibari—one of the most acclaimed enka singers and a cultural icon in postwar Japan—got married in 1962, she temporarily reduced her professional activities at her husband's wish, fully returning to working only after having divorced two years later (Kobayashi 2001). The immensely popular 1970s' idol Yamaguchi Momoe, on the other hand, declared that she would "selfishly" choose private happiness over public success and completely retired with her marriage in 1980 (Ogura 1989, 40). In fact, one of the few acceptable reasons for women singers to quit and end their "public service" as performers was marriage. This was exemplified by the popular idol trio, the Candies. Their decision to break up in 1978 against their management's wishes caused controversy because, instead of marriage, it was motivated by their wish to "return to being ordinary girls" (Katō 1979, 46–7).

The archetypical housewife was also constantly articulated in popular song lyrics (Zettsu 2002, 22–3). A prominent example is the male singer-songwriter Sada Masashi's hit "Kanpaku Declaration" (Kanpaku sengen, 1979), in which a husband-to-be impresses on his fiancée all her obligations as a wife, such as cooking, child-rearing, and taking care of her beauty.[3] When "Kanpaku Declaration" was released, it was read as good-natured humor about women's and men's "natural" roles (Zettsu 2002, 26). But while the lyrics humorously depict (even mock) the useless man who has to depend on his wife in the domestic sphere, they also effectively underline the normative gender-based labor divide and the husband's role as the head of the household:

There are things that only you can do
For everything else, just follow me without objections

Sada's lyrics exemplify a broader issue in contemporary Japan: the binary division of gender roles effectively placed many women in a subordinate position (e.g., Ochiai 1996; Shiota 2000). This tendency can also be observed in many popular song lyrics. Whereas the power relation in Sada's song is exceptionally explicit, many other songs communicate a hierarchy between genders much more implicitly.

According to separate analyses of gender representations in Japanese popular song by linguist Jugaku Akiko and literary scholar Zettsu Tomoyuki, popular songs of the 1970s often placed female characters in relation to men—usually a loved one, occasionally a father. These women were portrayed as having romantic dreams about becoming a bride or a mother, dwelling in loneliness without a man, crying after a breakup or after being cheated on, and being careful not to make a bad impression on her love interest. They were waiting, crying, apologizing, and promising to give up everything—including their personalities—for a man (Jugaku 1979, 104–36; Zettsu 2002). Such lyrics reproduced the binary expectations of gender roles by imagining women's actions, positions, and opinions in a manner that limited their individual agency (Take 1999, 169). Although there were naturally exceptions to this rule, the stereotypical image of women echoed the common expectation in which they would take a back seat for a man (*otoko o tateru*).[4]

Yamaguchi Momoe's songs, for example, objectified her by presenting her as young and innocent while containing sexual undertones and stating her willingness to devote herself to a man. In Yamaguchi's smash hit, "The Experience of One Summer" (Hitonatsu no keiken, 1974), the protagonist promises to give her loved one "the most precious thing of a girl." This was largely understood to mean her virginity (Sakai 2013, 46–7). Apart from sexualizing the fifteen-year-old Yamaguchi, the song also expresses the protagonist's devotion to serve her loved one by prioritizing his wishes:

I protected it to devote it to my loved one
It doesn't matter if I get dirty or if I cry; love is so precious

"Green Fruit" (Aoi kajitsu, 1973), an earlier hit, is even more straightforward in presenting Yamaguchi as passive and inexperienced but emotionally devoted and sexually available. In the lyrics, everything depends on the man's will, and the heroine is ready to taint her reputation as a woman in order to please him:

If you want, you can do anything to me
I don't even mind if they spread rumors that I'm not a good girl

The male-centric nature of such songs perhaps seems inevitable in a music industry that was dominated by male producers and songwriters, who often constructed women's images to appeal to the assumed preferences of male audiences (Igarashi 1999, 105). However, especially when performed by female singers, the songs also created an illusion about representing women's viewpoints and experiences. Even if the audiences did not passively embrace the illusion as such, the continuous repetition of similar performances created a framework that suggested accepted models of behavior for different genders (cf. Lieb 2013, 13). Echoing Judith Butler's argument about gender being "performatively constituted by the 'expressions' that are said to be its results" (Butler 1999, 33), the feminist media scholar Inoue Teruko notes:

Although women do not entirely depend on the media, they create their ways of life and form their perspectives while, to a certain extent, using media as a reference. Women's images in the media are not merely depictions of how women *should be* but also construct the *reality* of women's representations. (Inoue 2009, 2)

As a ubiquitous presence on television and an omnipresent part of everyday culture, kayōkyoku was a prominent site for projecting such images (cf. Hase & Ōta 2007).[5] Thus, the ordinary lifespan of a female kayōkyoku singer in 1970s Japan can be read as a large-scale performance of conventional gender roles. The singer first sang about fictional romance in terms mainly defined by men, eventually found real-life romance, got married, and quit professional life. Through continuous repetition in the media, popular songs constituted a powerful site to maintain gender norms. For this reason, Zettsu Tomoyuki has called kayōkyoku "the strongest form of thought" in postwar Japan (Zettsu 2002, 8–9).

Ironically, the female singers who performed these songs were often given authorship-like status in their work because of the strength of their performance (cf. Warwick 2007, 94–6). This especially pertains to widely idolized enka stars such as Misora Hibari and Fuji Keiko: they were commonly celebrated as geniuses whose personal voices and dramatic life stories influenced their songs and public images. Even though these images were at least partly constructed by male lyricists and producers, it was the performer—the successful working woman—whom the audience admired.

However, several women singers have later revealed that they felt uncomfortable with their public images and wanted to quit because their production restricted their agency and downplayed their aspirations as performers. One of them was Yamaguchi Momoe, who subsequently stated that her sexualized image, while contributing to her popularity, negatively impacted her motivation to perform (Tsutsumi 2000, 49). In this, the positions of many singers perhaps echoed the feminist music scholar Susan McClary's observations about opera in the past: while allowing women to excel on the stage, the music, libretti, and production by men fundamentally rendered opera "a discourse that offers up the female as spectacle while guaranteeing that she will not step out of line" (McClary 2002, 152).

Conversely, a contesting viewpoint can participate in dissolving gender stereotypes in the media (Muramatsu 2002, 74).[6] In television and print media, such viewpoints were typically provided by female creators, who began to gain a stronger foothold in the male-dominated media industries around the mid-1970s (Inoue 2009). Early examples in popular music, although relatively few in number, date to the 1960s. Producer Watanabe Misa, who co-founded the influential Watanabe Production with her husband in 1959, is an example of a highly successful female producer. Iwatani Tokiko, Yasui Kazumi, and Arima Mieko were some of the few successful women lyricists who worked for the kayōkyoku industry before the 1970s.[7] Iwatani, who translated or wrote original lyrics for over 3,000 songs from the 1950s onwards, is considered one of the most influential Japanese lyricists for her highly successful work for artists such as the Peanuts, Kayama Yūzō, and Gō Hiromi.

While female lyricists were not uniform in voice, their lyrics tended not to objectify women, portray them in hierarchical relationships, or downplay their independence to the extent of the examples discussed above (cf. Jugaku 1979; Zettsu 2002). Many songs also negotiated the ideals for female characters, subtly contesting the portrayals of women who just passively devoted themselves to men. A prominent example is the Peanuts' smash hit "Love Vacation" (Koi no bakansu, 1963). Iwatani's lyrics focus on a romance, but the heroine is not depicted as blindly following her loved one. Unlike the protagonists in Yamaguchi Momore's songs, she takes an active stance in their relationship. Whether the "nakedness" in the lyrics refer to emotional self-revelation or sexual desire remains open to interpretation, but in either case, the heroine articulates her own will:

On the hot sand that shines golden
Let's fall in love, naked like a mermaid and a merman

The late 1960s also saw the debuts of several women singers who wrote some of their songs themselves, such as Katō Tokiko, Moriyama Ryōko, and Asakawa Maki. Although occasionally mentioned as the "first Japanese female singer-songwriters" (Nagai 2013, 106–7), the majority of their songs were still written by male songwriters. Nevertheless, the work of these early women songwriters was pioneering in diversifying portrayals of women in popular songs and foregrounding women's agency in musical production. Both aspects foreshadowed developments in the 1970s, and this is when Yuming's role becomes critical. Her professional debut as a songwriter on Kahashi Katsumi's album in 1971 was a prelude to a momentous change that soon swept over Japanese popular music.

The Rise of Women Singer-Songwriters

In April 1972, the fifteen-year-old Taniyama Hiroko released her debut album *It's So Pleasantly Quiet* (Shizuka de ii na). Soon thereafter, the eighteen-year-old Yuming released her debut single. Only a few months later, the 21-year-old Itsuwa Mayumi released her debut album *Girl* (Shōjo), which had been recorded in Los Angeles with such influential musicians as Carole King and David Campbell. In 1973, the sixteen-year-old Kosaka Akiko was awarded the grand prix of the Yamaha World Popular Song Festival with "You, My Dear" (Anata), and the same year, the nineteen-year-old Yuming released her debut album *Vapor Trail*. As stylistically different as these musicians were, they were connected by one aspect: all of them were young women who wrote the music and lyrics for their songs.

This change was revolutionary. At last, mainstream popular music in Japan was seeing a wave of women's voices in songwriting (Lehtonen 2021). The first Yuming boom of the mid-1970s in particular is often credited for popularizing the female singer-songwriter in the music industry (Take 1999, 176; Nagai 2013, 6). After this performer category had been firmly established, the latter half of the 1970s saw the debuts of dozens of highly popular female singer-songwriters, including Nakajima Miyuki, Takeuchi Mariya, Yano Akiko, Yagami Junko, Ozaki Amii, Ōnuki Taeko, and Yoshida Minako—to name but a few. Apart from triumphing commercially, their creative skills were also widely recognized and celebrated in the media: Yuming was commonly characterized as a "genius," whereas Takeuchi

Mariya was even called the "savior" of Japanese popular music (Shūkan myōjō 1978b; Matsutōya 1984, 8–9). Soon after the mid-1970s, rankings of the most prominent Japanese singer-songwriters always included several women (e.g., Aono 1976; Mimi 1977)—a situation that would have been impossible to even imagine only a few years earlier!

Young women welcomed this change. Yuming and Nakajima Miyuki in particular are often mentioned as cultural icons who expressed different images of femininity in their songs, providing their audiences with models that had previously not existed in popular music. In an article about the two, journalist Shimazaki Kyōko explains that encountering their songs in her youth was an eye-opening experience for her, because they incorporated a new model of womanhood: "I experienced an awakening when I saw these women singing about larger themes than romance or the world within the radius of three meters" (Shimazaki 2006, 86). By "the radius of three meters," Shimazaki refers to the average size of a room in a Japanese house, that is, life within the domestic sphere. Comparing Yuming's and Nakajima's significance to women writers of the Heian period (794–1185), Shimazaki notes that their music demonstrated that women were entitled to goals other than what society was pushing on them.[8]

Shimazaki's observation is best exemplified by female singer-songwriters' songs with symbolic, poetic lyrics that picture heroines who are deeply philosophical about life. For example, Itsuwa Mayumi's "Girl" (Shōjo, 1972) expresses the thoughts and anxieties of a girl at the threshold of adulthood. She is watching how time passes on the other side of a fence (that is, in the world of adulthood):

The girl knew that one day
She would have to cross the fence from which blew a cold wind

The charm of Itsuwa's lyrics lies in their wordings open to interpretation. Although the keywords "girl" and "passing time" evoke one's road to adulthood, I have also seen interpretations suggesting that the protagonist is afraid of death—or even planning suicide. The song could also be read as an expression of the anxiety one experiences before a significant change in life, or more specifically, the social pressures that women must face when entering adulthood. Whatever interpretation one chooses to follow, Itsuwa approached this universal theme from a woman's viewpoint, which was a notable contrast with the conventional portrayals of dependent female characters.

A similarly universal theme is addressed in Taniyama Hiroko's "The Milky Way Will Keep On Rotating" (Gingakei wa yappari mawatteru, 1972), which cynically ponders the meaninglessness of life and political idealism, and the powerlessness of an individual in the big world. This approach resembles the more nihilistic folk songs of the early 1970s, such as Inoue Yōsui's iconic "I Haven't Got an Umbrella" (Kasa ga nai, 1972), which was released about the same time as Taniyama's song. Each verse ends with lines that underline the smallness of humans in the universe:

Even if the Earth would disappear
The Milky Way will keep of rotating

By contrast, Nakajima Miyuki's "Era" (Jidai, 1975) is a much more comforting song about the ways in which positive times will always follow darker periods in life. While "Era" is a typical "cheering song" (ōenka) to help someone along, its worldview also echoes philosophical and religious concepts about the circularity of time:

Circulate, circulate, the eras circulate
Repeating joy and sadness
Even the lovers who parted today
Will be reborn and will meet each other again

Not all lyrics by female singer-songwriters challenged conventional gender roles. For example, Kosaka Akiko's "You, My Beloved" has been described as a quintessential idealization of the housewife because of its romantic dreaming about domestic life (Zettsu 2002, 23). However, this simply demonstrates that women songwriters portrayed women in diverse ways (cf. Take 1999, 168–70). As Shimazaki Kyōko's praise of Yuming and Nakajima suggests, it was important for female singer-songwriters to be publicly recognized as *authors*. Recognition as an author underlined their agency as creative women both in public discussion and within the music industry. Therefore, the individual authorship embedded in the image of New Music also helped to foster women musicians' *collective* agency.

Yuming's immense popularity in particular made the female singer-songwriter into a marketable concept in the mid-1970s; virtually all younger female singer-songwriters were compared to her, even if they strongly denied any influence. Another reason for the music industry to pivot toward women was the international success of female singer-songwriters like Carole King and Joni Mitchell. Yuming even speculated that Murai Kunihiko, who admired King's music, produced her debut because he saw this trend in the United States and wanted to make her "the Japanese Carole King" (Chikushi 1984, 202). Despite parallels, however, Yuming never referred to her foreign counterparts as role models; instead, she mentioned British male rock groups, such as Led Zeppelin, King Crimson, and Procol Harum (Matsutōya 1984, 91). A similar stance also concerned other women singer-songwriters, such as Itsuwa Mayumi and Takeuchi Mariya (Lehtonen 2021, 132).

Perhaps female singer-songwriters in New Music preferred to be considered among all musicians on the basis of their individual creativity rather than as "women musicians." In any case, their emergence as a phenomenon coincided with the rise of women's movements, and with it, attention on feminist discussions in the media. Some writers have drawn a parallel between developments in popular music and those in the larger social sphere, suggesting that the two were interlinked (Take 1999, 170). But what were the connections between the two, if any?

Women's Liberation

The early 1970s saw the foundation of many feminist groups. These anti-establishment groups inherited the activist stance from New-Left political associations of the late 1960s: using strong language, they called for a fundamental change to the entire social system, which, they argued, exploited the family structure and binary gender roles for the sake of capitalistic profit-making (Shigematsu 2012). This marked the launch of the Japanese women's liberation movement (*ūman ribu*).[9]

At first, the women's liberation movement did not gain widespread approval in mainstream circles. By the mid-1970s, however, many women who felt oppressed by the male-centered society began to openly address gender-based discrimination. After the United Nations declared the Decade for Women in 1975, Japanese governmental organizations started collaborating with more moderate feminist groups that did not necessarily wish to overturn the social system but were invested in fostering more possibilities for women's active participation in the public sphere. As Ehara Yumiko observes, this development signified "shifts from the movement to institutions, from activists to scholars, and from newsletters with limited circulation to mainstream journalism" (Ehara 1993, 50).

This change in the mid-1970s marked a division of *radical* and *liberal* feminisms, the former represented by anti-establishment activists and the latter by more moderate groups that collaborated with state organizations. As explained by Setsu Shigematsu, *radical feminism* was based on political activism; demanded "comprehensive political, economic, and cultural transformations"; derived its ideologies from earlier leftist activists; and used confrontational language. By contrast, more moderate *liberal feminism* was not so confrontational; it did not necessarily call for fundamental social reform but instead endorsed institutional and legislative changes that would promote women's emancipation within existing social structures (Shigematsu 2012, xix; cf. Kearney 2017, 25–8).

Although the mainstream media originally ridiculed radical feminism, they began to support liberal feminist goals after the mid-1970s, publishing articles that celebrated career women and women's participation in the public sphere (Ochiai 1996, 85–7). The positive image of independent women soon coined a buzzword: "soaring women" (*tonderu onna*). Soaring women (1) were economically independent; (2) possessed skills and genius that were publicly recognized; (3) could work like men; (4) thought for themselves and asserted their viewpoints; and (5) were ideologically progressive (Asahi shinbun 1980, 15). As these characterizations reveal, "successful women" were largely defined by masculine standards, such as professional devotion and assertiveness. In this way, the discourse on soaring women was in fact not aligned with the arguments of many feminists, who did not wish women to be like men (Ochiai 1996, 89). Nevertheless, the media put up "soaring women" in politics, the arts, and entertainment as examples for women to pursue in an ideal society. This contributed to the discussion about an "age of women" (*onna no jidai*) that had purportedly begun with the Decade for Women (Mackie 2003, 168).

Eventually, liberal feminism became a trend in the media and was branded as a commercial concept: the social agency of women became equated with their freedom to consume as individuals. According to many feminist scholars, this commercialization—a typical development in capitalist societies to make potential threats less dangerous—diluted the anti-capitalist and collective goals of radical feminism (Shigematsu 2005). Yet the focus on individuality also diversified the images of women in the media, which tilted away from automatically associating womanhood with homemaking and motherhood:

[I]ntentional or not, since the 1970s, apart from women's
magazines, […] media like girls' comics and popular
songs have dissolved models for binary gender roles and
encouraged the emergence of women who are not mothers,
homemakers, or wives, but individuals. In this way, such
media in which the creators and receivers are relatively close
to each other act like a mirror reflecting the minds of people
in different times. (Inoue 2009, 5)

That the creator and receiver were "relatively close to each
other" by being women was instrumental for this change, for it
made possible the wider dissemination of women's voices. This
development draws a parallel with the emergence of female
singer-songwriters. As popular, economically independent, and
celebrated individual authors with an elevated level of agency,
they represented the epitome of "soaring women" and were
often referred to as such in the media. Writing lyrics that were
in a woman's actual voice, their work challenged conventional
images of women in popular music and diversified the images
of women in the larger media world.

However, Japanese female songwriters were not automatically all "feminists," nor did they necessarily write songs with
a political aim in mind. Many female singer-songwriters adopted
a vocabulary echoing that of earlier male lyricists, particularly
when they later became involved with the kayōkyoku industry
and wrote songs for idol singers. Many female singer-
songwriters also distinguished between their own songs and
those they wrote for kayōkyoku singers. Yuming, for example,
often used the pen name Kureta Karuho (a wordplay on Greta
Garbo) when writing idol songs that she "would not sing herself"

(Shūkan myōjō 1982, 42), and Takeuchi Mariya stated that the songs she wrote for idols were different from the ones she wrote for herself (Kamidate 2019). This compartmentalization between songs they wrote for idols and those for themselves suggests that many women singer-songwriters worked pragmatically as professional songwriters under the constraints of the system, rather than acting as musician-activists who channeled their art to fight for equality among genders.

For example, while Yuming's, Itsuwa's, Taniyama's, and Nakajima's lyrics discussed above subtly challenged conventional gender roles, their work differed considerably from the overtly feminist songs by the blues singer-songwriter Kobayashi Mariko. Kobayashi explicitly addressed gender inequality in her work, identified as a feminist, and made music to "irritate men" (Chiharu and Aizawa 2020, 137–40). Using confrontative language and actively engaging with radical feminism, she sang about sexual abuse of women in songs such as "Rape Feeling" (1978) and "Toilet Blues" (Benjo no burūsu, 1978).[10] Her work was thus closer to politically engaged folk of the late 1960s and radical feminism than to commercial New Music and liberal feminism. Kobayashi's political language is exemplified in "Rape Feeling" (translated in Chiharu and Aizawa 2020, 140):

Guys always want to rape us.
They have this desire without their knowledge. [...]
So do we let them do it, or do we stop them?
No More Rape!

As this comparison demonstrates, New Music was disconnected from radical feminism and was typically not explicitly articulating a feminist ideal. However, while not directly linked to women's movements, female singer-songwriters in New Music did symbolize the goals of liberal feminism: through female songwriters, New Music showed a woman's world through a woman's eyes and afforded her agency. Furthermore, New Music remotely shared the same roots as feminism in the activism of the 1960s, and the broader media discourses may have directed more attention to female artists and contributed to their support in the music industry. These genealogies are clarified in Figure 4.1 (page 82), which presents liberal feminism and New Music in a continuum of establishmentarianism and commercialism.

By the time of Kobayashi's debut in 1978, feminism had already been branded as a commercial concept, and her songs were generally considered too radical. They were eventually rejected by other feminists, and Kobayashi quit making music in 1982 after being physically attacked in a live performance (Chiharu and Aizawa 2020, 141). Her example demonstrates that although women had become increasingly prominent in the music industry, female imagery, topics, and roles were still prescribed according to restrictions that society placed on women. This is also exemplified by the discussion surrounding *The 14th Moon* as Yuming's swan song.

The 14th Moon and Yuming's Retirement

Although Yuming denied any intention of ending her career in 1976, she revealed in retrospect that she had indeed originally decided to retire as a performing artist with the release of *The*

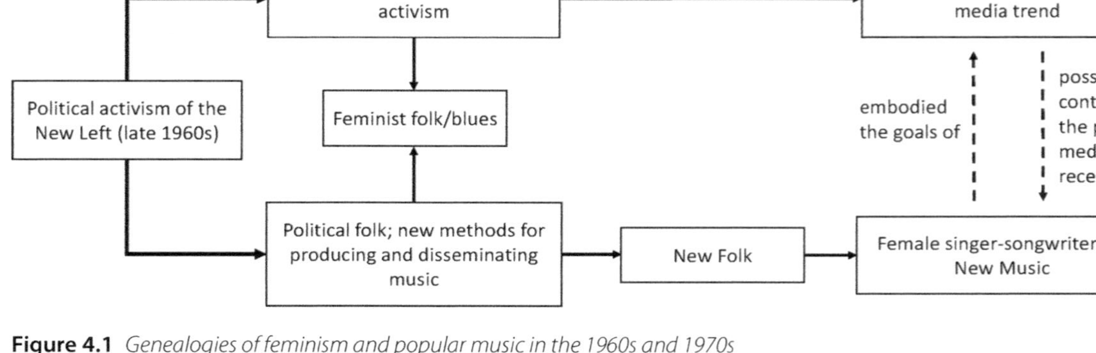

Figure 4.1 *Genealogies of feminism and popular music in the 1960s and 1970s*

14th Moon and her marriage (Matsutōya 1984, 116–22). To be more precise, she intended to keep on writing songs for other performers while working primarily as a housewife (Matsutōya 2011, 9). Even so, her decision to withdraw from public life was in line with the general practices of that time. The expectation that women retire with marriage was in fact so normative that when kayōkyoku singers Yamaguchi Momoe and Minami Saori got married and ended their careers against their management companies' wishes, they were characterized as "soaring women" for expressing their own will (Katō 1979, 46–7). In other words, female musicians could be performers answering to producers or wives answering to husbands.

In Yuming's case, it was not Matsutōya Masataka who pressed her to end her career, though. He stated in several interviews after their marriage that he would wish for Yuming to keep on making music and would be happy to share domestic work with her (Myōjō 1977a)—a stance practically unheard of for upper-middle-class Japanese men like Matsutōya (cf. Ueno 1988, 179). Instead of her fiancé, it was the media that influenced Yuming's decision by expecting women musicians to be what Kristin J. Lieb calls "short-term brands": singers who perform only for a couple of years (Lieb 2013, 40–2). Certain of Yuming's retirement, the media in 1976 anticipated the appearance of the "next Yuming" (or, as they wrote, "post-Yuming") long before her wedding (Shūkan myōjō 1976c). Above, I quoted Inoue Teruko's argument that the continuous repetition of certain gender models in the media effectively turned these images into reality. This is precisely what happened to Yuming, who later revealed that she felt so offended by the speculations in the media that they impacted her decision to retire:

> When the recording for *The 14th Moon* ended, I decided that I would quit making music—at the same time as I entered into marriage, that is.
> Isn't it so that one is considerably affected by the voices around her? When I heard someone talk about "post-Yuming," I felt so disgraced. It was as if they buried Yuming while she was still alive. (Matsutōya 1984, 116–17)

The 14th Moon was about transformation in many ways, and as we have seen, these transformations formed parallels with wider social developments. But did the album also reflect the gender issues of its time—either by reproducing the expectations imposed on women or by challenging them? This question can only be answered by addressing the album from the viewpoint of women's roles.

5 Soaring Women

Perhaps I represent a backstage version of women's liberation.

– YUMING (CHIKUSHI 1984, 54)

In 1979, Yuming started a new serial in the *Shinpyō* magazine.[1] Titled "Yuming's Talk with Women," she invited well-known women across different fields of culture to discuss their work, society, philosophy—anything that happened to cross their minds. Yuming's second guest was Michishita Kyōko, a feminist video artist, novelist, and translator who was a prominent proponent of the women's liberation movement. In the early 1970s, for example, Michishita produced the videotape *Being Women in Japan: Liberation Within My Family*, which now belongs to the collections of the Museum of Modern Art in New York.

In their discussion, Michishita commended Yuming as an example of what women could achieve:

> [I] wish for a lot of women like you to come forward as exemplars—that is, women who can show that they are living their own lives and that it means living life to its fullest. [...] Among these kinds of women, you are number one—so I hope that you continue to put out the splendid parts of your work in front of different kinds of women and men, demonstrating that you are living such a fun, beautiful, and interesting life. (Matsutōya and Michishita 1979, 109)

Later evaluations have largely echoed Michishita's recognition of Yuming as a "soaring woman." The nonfiction writer Yanagisawa Takeshi, for example, has defined Yuming as a "woman who created an era" (Yanagisawa 2011), whereas the music critic Take Hideki equated her success with the rise of women's movements (Take 1999, 173). As positive as these characterizations are, they tend to focus solely on Yuming's public image. But what about her music? Did anything in her songs embody these characteristics?

If we ask contemporary audiences, the answer appears to be yes. Even before the first Yuming boom, she was characterized as a musician embodying "girls' dreams" (Yomiuri shinbun 1974, 5). More importantly, many women have subsequently elaborated on the impact that her work had on their lives in their youth. The psychologist and feminist writer Ogura Chikako described Yuming's songs as revolutionary, in that they offered an alternative to the "conservativism" in many male musicians' songs (Ogura 1989, 181). The leader of the Social Democratic Party of Japan, Fukushima Mizuho, characterized Yuming's way of encouraging women to find their own lifestyles as "soft feminism" (Fukushima 2014). Journalist Shimazaki Kyōko believed that Yuming's music specifically channeled women's aspirations (Shimazaki 2006, 86). According to essayist Sakai Junko, Yuming encouraged young Japanese women to have their own dreams. For these women and Sakai herself, Yuming's songs changed their lives (Sakai 2013, 18).

As shown by these examples, Yuming's music gave many women a model rarely available in kayōkyoku, folk, and rock. In this, her songs parallel the feminist media scholar Inoue

Teruko's conceptualization of "women's media" (*josei media*)—media created for women. As Inoue explains, women's media offered alternatives to the mainstream media industry (*shuryū media*), such as so-called general-audience television programs, magazines, and newspapers, in which women's images were constructed mainly by men. Inoue mentions girls' and women's manga, women's magazines, romantic novels, and television dramas as the most typical examples of women's media. Therefore, the concept should not be understood as a unified and singular culture for "all women" regardless of age and social class, nor does it necessarily reflect women's lived experiences; rather, it is a loose media genre whose primary target audiences and creators are connected by their gender. Nevertheless, by focusing on women as individuals, commercial women's media also helped to diversify women's images in the media at large (Inoue 2009).

Considering how strongly Inoue's discussion about women's media echoes the observations about women singer-songwriters' work in the previous chapter, it may seem surprising that her list does not include popular music. However, this has to do with the target audiences. Unlike the media products that mainly targeted women, popular music in the 1970s did not typically incorporate such gender-specific divisions. Rock, folk, and kayokyoku certainly held different meanings for listeners of different genders, but their primary audiences were more typically segregated by age, ideology, and social class. For example, a survey conducted by the Japanese national broadcasting company NHK in 1978 suggests that while women in all age groups were more likely to listen to pop than men and men listened to enka more than women, audiences were otherwise not that strongly divided by gender (NHK 1979).[2] Also Yuming intended her work for audiences of all genders (Ren'ai kajin kenkyūkai 1996, 172–4).

In order to examine Yuming's work in the context of women's media and mainstream media, I expand the use of "women's media" to include music made *by* women, even if the intended audience was not so specifically defined as in the media genres listed by Inoue. This conceptualization is informed by a question Inoue presented in the early 1980s: "Do the images of women [...] disseminated by the media dominate women's consciousness, or conversely, does the consciousness of modern women [...] create media culture?" (Inoue 1981, 114). Considering the music industry in the 1970s, it was important that Yuming was in a creative position, as this allowed her to articulate viewpoints that male songwriters typically did not write about.

This is not to say that Yuming's music would have represented a collective "women's voice" in the 1970s. As her characterization as "the most *crystal* woman" (Chapter 3) implies, her music tended to communicate the ideals of a middle-class, urban, heterosexual, cisgender, and ethnically Japanese woman, whose work spoke especially to listeners in their late teens and early twenties (Suzuki 1976, 57). However, in the contemporary discourse that emphasized a binary division between women and men, Yuming could negotiate the restrictions and expectations that public discourse tended to place on women at large (cf. Muramatsu 2002; Ueno 2012). Her position in between women's media (as a female creator) and mainstream media (in which her work was widely disseminated) potentially enabled her to integrate new viewpoints into the mainstream. To better understand this aspect of *The 14th Moon*, let us begin by examining how Yuming portrayed the heroines of her songs.

Independent Heroines

Several years after the release of *The 14th Moon*, Yuming revealed that with the title song, she wished to present an alternative portrayal of women in popular music:

> Until then, love songs were all about broken hearts or romance, and songs with unassertive women were considered good. Many songs followed a pattern where the woman's will was not clear. As women had not been granted the freedom to act as they please in love songs until then, I wanted to make a more self-assured song. That's how I wrote "The 14th Moon." (in Sakai 2013, 46)

Recall that "The 14th Moon" describes its heroine preparing to confess her love—hardly a radical or challenging portrayal. But when compared with conventional lyrics where a man's will defines the thoughts and acts of women, Yuming's self-assertive heroine did present an alternative: a desiring subject who is not afraid to express her own will in a situation that was commonly thought of as requiring a man's initiative. For this reason, Sakai Junko argues that "The 14th Moon" should be understood as a celebration of women's independence (Sakai 2013, 47).

What about the other songs? To examine the roles that Yuming gives her heroines, I will next compare the lyrics of *The 14th Moon* with Jugaku Akiko's observations about women's typical roles in popular songs in the 1970s. Jugaku's analysis lists women characters' most typical *actions* (crying for a man and promising to stay beside him); *expressions of dependence* (waiting for, snuggling up to, and following a man); *descriptions of appearance* (long hair, cuteness); and *desires* (willingness to serve and devote oneself to a man). When referring to themselves, women characters often used expressions by which they run themselves down, such as no-good, weak, and dumb (Jugaku 1979, 107–33). To examine how Yuming challenged these portrayals, I discuss the heroines of *The 14th Moon* in five categories that represent different aspects of the protagonists' independence: (1) cool; (2) willful; (3) growing; (4) introspective; and (5) longing. These categories are not exclusive—virtually all of them overlap with the others in some way—but most songs can be classified by the primary type of the heroine's stance.

The first category, *cool*, contains heroines who are responding to the end of a love affair with feelings that may be unexpected for that situation. Sakai Junko appreciated that Yuming's songs depicted women who refused to cry when they broke up with their boyfriends, as they challenged the social paradigm that women were incomplete without a man and, by extension, a family. In Sakai's view, these songs thus suggested that it was acceptable, even cool, for women to focus on themselves instead of being invested in finding love to fulfill their social obligations (Sakai 2013, 26–9).[3] These heroines refuse some of the typical actions (crying) and desires (devoting oneself) for women, as observed in Jugaku's analysis.

"Ripples" is a song of this type. Its heroine is lying on a boat, reading a collection of short stories. She has come here alone to reminisce about the happy days with her boyfriend. Instead of crying over heartbreak, she revels in *not* knowing the current state of their relationship:

Bridge 1: Without checking whether our love has ended
I came here alone and I'm glad

She is not running away, however, as she acknowledges that the relationship is over. Here, the song connects her stance to the overarching theme of the album by suggesting that the relationship now belongs to the past and, if continued, would disturb the natural development of things. The heroine expresses her decision to move on:

Bridge 2: Had I patched up a love affair that's ending,
I would have delayed myself from living for tomorrow

It is only in the bridges where the heroine directly addresses the end of her relationship. Here, the music seems to contradict her "coolness," instead suggesting an aspect of melancholy by modulating from C major to C minor. But this notion is as temporary as the ripples going through the heroine's fingers: the modulation back to major before the end of the bridges suggests that musing on the end of her relationship only adds to the heroine's resolution about the preferability of the current situation. Enjoying "her own October," she expresses her independence, saying that she is perfectly fine with not finding love for some time.

A similar type of independence concerns the heroines of the second category, *willful*. They are not afraid to assert their own viewpoints—again a notable difference with the conventional portrayals of women, as observed in Jugaku's analysis. We already saw that the heroine of "The 14th Moon" is an example of this stance. Another example is "Sun Shower," in which the heroine's boyfriend has gone surfing without her to Chigasaki (a coastal town popular among surfers). The heroine has decided to follow her boyfriend by train and is now accompanying him on the beach. She may first appear to be the opposite of willful. She craves more attention from her boyfriend and is outwardly apologetic about coming to the beach, knowing that she is only "getting in the way." Finally, she notes:

You don't have to be kind; be the cool way you are but just stay beside me

But we should not be deceived by what the heroine says (or imagines saying) to her boyfriend. The lyrics do not focus on accommodating his wishes but on expressing the heroine's determination and subjective emotions. She is not passive, nor is she changing herself or the way she acts: she accompanies her boyfriend without waiting for him to ask, following him to the beach on her own and not taking no for an answer. Whereas one of the most typical lines in songs for female singers in the 1970s was "I will stay beside you" (Jugaku 1979, 110), "Sun Shower" turns this conventional expression of women's devotion around by transforming it to a command—given to a man! In this context, the last line can be read much more assertively: the heroine is telling her boyfriend never to go without her again.

A different brand of willfulness is displayed by the heroines of the third category, *growing*. In both songs of this type, "Where Does Loneliness Go" and "Good Luck and Goodbye," the heroine meets a loved one from her past. This situation puts her in between the past and the present and forces her to undergo a transformation on an emotional level. Therefore, the name of this category refers to a specific way in which its heroines find themselves encountering contradictory emotions but eventually arrive at a resolution that liberates them from the tension between the past and the present.

In "Where Does Loneliness Go," the past loved one is now living abroad and wants to meet the heroine while visiting Japan. She still holds onto the emotions of the time before he had left:

Don't laugh at me, even if I still cherish
How you told me I'm OK just the way I am

Whatever hopes the heroine had for their reunion, however, they are never met. Ultimately, she notes that he has become someone who does not belong to her life (*tanin*): feeling that something inside her has "really come to an end," she decides to let go of him and her past emotions.

In the more optimistic "Good Luck and Goodbye," the heroine happens to see her former boyfriend while strolling in the city. Although their relationship did not end on good terms, she now feels little pain:

It was a love that hurt me, but no trace of that remains
Although I thought that if we were to meet by chance, I would start crying

The heroine becomes immersed in the contradictory emotions that the unexpected situation arouses: although the two are now in new relationships, she suddenly finds herself hoping that he would see her bus off. But in the end, she understands that everything between them is over, and she writes the words "good luck and goodbye" to the window of the bus as a farewell to him.

The *growing* heroines resemble their *cool* counterparts in that they acknowledge, without excess drama, that their romance has come to an end. These songs revisit a breakup at a later stage, when the protagonist has already moved on to other lovers. She acknowledges her past pain and looks upon her former lover with nostalgia. In other words, she accepts the past and moves on instead of desperately clinging to her past loved one (cf. Take 1999, 169).

In this respect, the growing heroines also share similarities with the *introspective* ones. As discussed earlier, "Like Nothing Ever Happened" and "In the Morning Light" do not focus on romance but on memories, loss, and anxiety for the future. These songs parallel the heroines in the songs of Itsuwa Mayumi, Taniyama Hiroko, and Nakajima Miyuki, whose protagonists are deeply introspective about universal themes (Chapter 4).

By contrast, the heroines in the *longing* category of Yuming's songs are closer to conventional images of women who cannot stand being without their loved ones. However, I would argue that Yuming's songs incorporate a subtle yet important difference: her longing heroines are not feeling incomplete. As discussed earlier, the heroine of "Chuo Freeway" immerses herself in the pleasure of a drive and projects this moment onto a never-ending fantasy. Her longing is for the precious moment that will inevitably end with the exit off the freeway. In "A Summer Place," the heroine is at a holiday resort, waiting for her partner to return to their room. Her waiting aligns with Jugaku's analysis of kayōkyoku, in which women wait for their men as an expression of their devotion (Jugaku 1979, 117–18). While Yuming's heroine chides him for "ignoring her sighs," however, she is not feeling down without him; she fully expects him to return "before sunset" and is looking forward to that moment with anticipation. Her excitement is supported by the upbeat idiom of the song, which does not suggest melancholy.

While most other songs on the album also blend categories to some degree, the last song, "Late Summer (The Lonely Season)," is perhaps the best illustration of the limitations related to categorization as a means of analysis. I would classify the heroine as *introspective*: she compares life events with shifting seasons and objectively observes the flow of time. But at the same time, she also clearly finds herself in a *growing* position, having returned to her *furusato* that has remained the same while she has changed. The song also contains qualities from other categories: its title suggests *longing*, and since the heroine is remembering her past love without getting emotional, she is also *cool*. The only type the heroine does not represent is *willful*, as she remains an observer. Through this complexity, "Late Summer" acts as a natural epitaph to the album, as it summarizes many elements from the previous tracks and suggests both departure and continuation.

As varied as Yuming's heroines are, they are connected by one fundamental attribute: their independence. They do not define themselves or their positions in relation to their boyfriends, nor do they position themselves below men in the social hierarchy. When the heroine expresses her affection for her boyfriend, she is focused on *her* feelings and experiences rather than how he might be perceiving her. Most importantly, the heroines never change themselves for a man, nor do they swear their unconditional devotion to him (cf. Jugaku 1979; Zettsu 2002). While not radically feminist, they present a picture of an assertive, yet feminine woman, in keeping with liberal-feminist ideals.

To be sure, some details on *The 14th Moon* would allow for readings diverging from this independent image. Sakai Junko has noted that even though "The 14th Moon" depicts a willful heroine, she is sitting on the passenger seat and anticipates the reaction of her love interest. In other words, the man is the one who ultimately decides the direction, both for the car and for the relationship (Sakai 2013, 48). Nevertheless, the women "sitting on passenger seats" are not necessarily in subordinate positions; the man is also serving the heroine by taking the burden of driving from her shoulders. It is also important that Yuming's heroines have varying degrees of independence and assertiveness: according to Sakai, this diversity of perspectives supported a woman's choice to do what she pleased (Sakai 2013, 54). In fact, Yuming explicitly supported this stance in her discussion with Michishita Kyōko:

Michishita: [Women whose bodies are controlled by men] have turned into slaves. It's so mean, so unsightly.

Matsutōya: Yes, I agree.

Michishita: After all, I would wish this world to be based on a system where both women and men can choose a way of life that best suits their personal rhythm.

Matsutōya: Yup. And it's also okay if you can decide for yourself that you want to get married and raise children, isn't it? (Matsutōya and Michishita 1979, 109)

The negotiation of gender roles in the lyrics of *The 14th Moon* is not limited to its heroines but also concerns the spaces that the songs occupy. For example, both "The 14th Moon" and "Chuo Freeway" take place in cars. According to Fukami Haruka's observation, cars were most typically presented as masculine spaces that symbolized speed and action in Japanese popular culture in the early 1970s (Fukami 1989, 32–3). In contrast, Yuming's songs presented cars as a site for the expression of women's emotional worlds—a rendering that became popularized in Japanese City Pop a few years later (cf. Sommet 2020, 22–3). But did such negotiations concern other aspects of *The 14th Moon*?

Gendered Expressions

In his survey of the history of Japanese popular music, music historian Kikuchi Kiyomaro makes an interesting observation about gender and musical style in New Music. After noting that New Music drew on international trends and presented these influences as a mix of various styles, Kikuchi distinguishes between music by different genders:

Female singer-songwriters began to stand out from the beginning of the New Music era. Male musicians obstinately held on to their stance as folk and rock singers, and even when the industry sold their music as New Music, they clung to their [earlier] style. [...] By contrast, women singer-songwriters adopted the [musically diverse] style of New Music from the beginning. (Kikuchi 2008, 248)

In reality, the phenomenon was not as strictly gendered as Kikuchi suggests; by the late 1970s, many male singer-songwriters such as Yamashita Tatsurō incorporated more stylistic diversity than men who had debuted as folk and rock artists. But it is also true that women such as Yuming, Itsuwa Mayumi, and Ozaki Amii experimented earlier with different musical idioms within individual albums and often declared stylistic boundaries needless (Music Life 1972, 189; Myōjō 1977b, 214).[4] While it would be essentialist to argue that the stylistic variety of *The 14th Moon* represents a specifically "feminine" aspect, Kikuchi's observation raises the question of what kinds of gender expressions the sound and musical style of the album incorporate.

As many studies have noted, musical sounds are (often unconsciously) perceived in gendered terms (Kitagawa 1999; McClary 2002). For example, we may associate higher singing voices with femininity and lower voices with masculinity because women on average have higher voices than men. Similarly, perceptions of musical styles link with notions of femininity and masculinity. In discourses about popular music, pop has stereotypically been associated with music by and for women, whereas rock has been considered a more masculine genre (Kearney 2017). Regardless of male listeners of pop and female rock musicians, this division also dominated the discourse about popular music in Japan in the 1970s (Inoue 1999, 60–3).

A similar identification concerns the sounds of musical instruments. According to a study by Takechi Yūko, sounds of "softer" instruments such as the flute, harp, and keyboards are commonly associated with femininity in Japan, whereas the more "aggressive" sounds of electric guitar, drums, and trumpet are considered more masculine; these associations are internalized already in childhood (Takechi 2005; cf. Warwick 2007, 6). These attributes are obviously not absolute, and many Japanese popular music acts have defied expectations or mixed the so-called masculine and feminine.[5] The gendered associations of instruments and musical sounds have also altered with time.

These ideas do, however, resonate with the ways in which Yuming's music has been received as "feminine." Several scholars argue that the kayōkyoku songs she composed renewed the genre by introducing a "feminine" expression to it (Ogawa 1988, 155; Nagai 2013, 141). For example, Yuming emphasized the keyboards, associated with women, instead of the masculine electric guitar (Inoue 1999, 77; Bourdaghs 2012, 181). Practically speaking, her complex chord progressions work better with keyboards than a guitar—but what matters is how these sounds are read. Music journalist Yuasa Manabu characterizes the sounds on *The 14th Moon* as "softer" compared with Yuming's earlier albums, because it emphasizes light, acoustic sounds over the pop-rock styles of her earlier work (Kirarasha 2003, 33). Would Yuasa, then, be saying that this album is more "feminine"? If so, what would that mean?

Music writers, both in Japan and elsewhere, have long considered women's music as more superficial, commercial, and visually focused than men's music (Kearney 2017, 21–5; Minamida et al. 2019, 70–1). Yuming would seem to represent several attributes that supposedly exemplify this superficiality: she was a commercially successful woman who characterized her music as "pop" (Heibon 1976, 44), emphasized the visual aspects of her performances and public image (Arai 1976b), and was specifically recognized as a "feminine" artist (Yomiuri shinbun 1974, 5). Why then, has she not been accused of inauthenticity?

As one response, her music was never purely pop, and her authorship made it authentic. In addition, members of Happy End participated on her early albums. As the popular music scholar Wajima Yūsuke has observed, the reputation of the band has often been harnessed to grant associated acts an aura of authenticity (Wajima 2004).

But Yuming also managed to establish a brand of authenticity that differed from male folk and rock musicians in the 1970s. Consider the commercial aspects of *The 14th Moon*. Most tracks were originally written for kayōkyoku singers, commercials, and television programs—spheres that many earlier rock and folk musicians shunned as arenas for commercialized (read: inauthentic) performances (Take 1999, 164–5). Only a couple of years earlier, the "prince of folk," Yoshida Takurō, was bashed for having betrayed the folk audience with his commercialist stance to music-making. He had violated folk music's egalitarian and non-conformist values by becoming a star singing about romance. After that, people would shout, "Go to hell," when Yoshida performed at folk venues (Take 1999, 140).

By contrast, women musicians in Japan are so strongly associated with commercialism that it can even be conceptualized as a kind of *authenticity* specific to female artists (Cogan & Cogan 2006). Commercialism was also part of Yuming's artistic brand: as a woman musician, she could easily exploit this "women's authenticity" without being accused of tainting her artistic integrity. At the same time, she drew on the authorship, emotion, and rock instrumentation that were more often associated with authenticity for male artists.

A similar negotiation concerns the visual aspects of *The 14th Moon*. As Yuming's photo was not on the cover, the album did not objectify her image as a consumable to be purchased in a record store (cf. Igarashi 1999, 99; Stevens 2008, 109–10). Yet a four-page photograph collection of Yuming included with the album certainly acknowledged the importance of the visual for female artists. This focus on the visual can, however, become a double-edged sword: while granting female musicians more visibility, it foregrounds women's appearance, which can take attention away from their creativity and musicianship (Lieb 2013, 153–6; Kearney 2017, 244–7). Japanese female singer-songwriters like Takeuchi Mariya and Okamura Takako experienced this in the early 1980s. Both agreed to their agencies' wishes to perform on kayōkyoku programs on television but later regretted it, saying that these shows emphasized their visual appeal over their music, which took their work in a different direction from their intentions (Lehtonen 2021, 121).

How is Yuming depicted in the photograph collection? What does it communicate about her image as an artist? As discussed in Chapter 2, the photographs range from casual situations to fantasy-like shots, presenting Yuming as an ordinary person on the one hand and as a cool fashion model on the other. In other words, the photographs are not based on stereotypically objectifying imagery: unlike many idol singers at that time, Yuming is not photographed in sexy or cute outfits, such as swimsuits (cf. Inoue 2009, 29). Equally important is that Yuming herself oversaw her visual presentation. She had been designing her own album art since *Vapor Trail* (Matsuki 2016, 145), but *The 14th Moon* is the first album where she is credited as the art director. Yuming also controlled her own image by deciding not to appear on kayōkyoku shows. In other words, she did not allow the producers and directors of these shows to construct her visual presentation (cf. Lehtonen 2021, 128).

Therefore, I would argue that the photographs were part of Yuming's authorship and the broader integration of visuality into her artist brand. By the time *The 14th Moon* was released, she was celebrated for combining her songwriting skills with her distinct fashion sense (Katsura 1976, 83) and for her skills in producing live performances that were "straight out of a fashion magazine" (Heibon 1976, 151). In foregrounding her fashions, Yuming played to the audience's desire for attractive female entertainers while avoiding the stereotypical association of female attractiveness with superficiality; her image was simply fashionable, sophisticated, and cool. In other words, her brand of authorship and authenticity concerned not only her music but also the visual aspects of her public image and performance.

These observations suggest that Yuming's New Music was constructed out of the allowance for "feminine" sounds, commercialism, and visuality as part of an authentic image.

As such, they support Kikuchi Kiyomaro's argument about the significance of female singer-songwriters' work in the genre. But was this significance recognized in the music industry? To what extent did Yuming's work reflect the position of women?

Musical Transformations

Over forty years after the release of *The 14th Moon*, feminist scholar Ayako Kano posed a question that has been asked countless times during the past decades: "Should one be optimistic or pessimistic about the future of Japanese feminisms?" (Kano 2018, 276). This question was also important in the 1970s. If all the hype about soaring women had changed Japanese society like many wished, Kano's question would have been unnecessary in 2018. However, later developments eventually countered some of the optimism in the late 1970s.

Liberal feminist groups that collaborated with state organizations demanded that gender-based discrimination should be rooted out with legislation. The Equal Employment Opportunity Law was enacted in 1986, at a time when women in the workforce were increasing. However, discrimination continued in the form of two different career tracks, which Vera Mackie calls "management track" and "clerical" work (Mackie 2003, 185). Male workers were typically channeled to the management track, which had good opportunities for professional development, whereas female workers were typically given clerical work, which paid less and consisted of routine office functions (Ueno 2009, 121).

Furthermore, the conventional paradigm about homemaking women turned out to be difficult to undo. Although more women have entered public life during the past few decades, they are still expected to take on the lion's share of housework and child-rearing (Gender Equality Bureau Cabinet Office 2021). In 2021, Japan ranked 120th out of 156 countries in the World Economic Forum's *Global Gender Gap Report*, which measures 4 key dimensions: "economic participation and opportunity, educational attainment, health and survival, and political empowerment" (World Economic Forum 2021).[6] While these dimensions may not necessarily measure women's actual well-being in Japan (Steel 2019), Japanese feminists today are still addressing many of the same issues as in the 1970s (Kano 2018).

What about popular music? Although female singer-songwriters like Yuming broadened the ways that women are depicted in popular songs, there are still many examples of pop artists today whose public images are constructed mainly by men in ways similar to the 1970s. Looking back, Yuming's work may be comparable to the escapist images of independent women that became popularized in 1970s women's media after feminism had been branded as a commercial concept. As Setsu Shigematsu explains, the "independent, cosmopolitan lifestyle" depicted in these magazines was not the reality that most women experienced, but this "slippage and contradiction between the image and reality" sparked a "desire for mobility and freedom of choice and the products that symbolized this lifestyle" (Shigematsu 2005, 564). If addressed critically, the "distant yet attainable" aura of Yuming's songs constructed a similar space of imagination, in which young women could liberate themselves from the restrictions of society when they had to face those restrictions in the real world. Sakai Junko felt ambivalent about Yuming precisely for this reason:

> When I think about it now, the glamor […] that Yuming showed us was an unattainable dream. […] By surrendering ourselves to the world of her songs, we were able to escape to a more wonderful world, and it felt like tomorrow would always be better than today.
>
> I think many people have mixed feelings about Yuming, thinking that "she gave me such great dreams" but at the same time, "if only I hadn't seen those dreams…" (Sakai 2013, 18)

Sakai dubs the creation of such an escapist world as Yuming's "sin." Yuming's image as a soaring woman was also called into question after her marriage:

> Many women were disappointed by the fact that Yuming— who had symbolized women's creativity and independence, and who supposedly personified a new lifestyle for women— discarded her family name and took her husband's name instead [also as a performer]. […] [T]hese fans felt betrayed by [her] middle-class conservatism. (Shimazaki 2006, 86)[7]

However, Yuming ultimately did not live up to the middle-class norm. While Sakai's and Shimazaki's criticisms show that women have perceived Yuming's songs and public image in complex and contradictory ways, *The 14th Moon* also exemplifies many significant changes that the music industry underwent in the 1970s with the influx of women creators.

To begin with, *The 14th Moon* never became the swan song it was originally intended to be. Yuming eventually continued after a short break, later confessing that she found her original intention to end her career to be a "huge mistake" (Matsutōya 2011, 19). Her decision to return to music-making was also a signal to the wider social sphere: in defying the expectations for women at that time, Yuming set an example for others in a similar situation. In the 1980s, it indeed became much more common for female singers to continue their careers after marrying and having children. In addition to singer-songwriters, kayōkyoku stars like Iwasaki Hiromi and Matsuda Seiko were similarly liberated (cf. Lehtonen 2021, 128).[8]

The 14th Moon also exemplified another important change that expanded the roles of women in music production. Around the time of its release, the kayōkyoku industry started to hire women as songwriters more frequently. Originally, the industry hired only singer-songwriters who were already popular performers, but later, it also started commissioning songs from women who themselves had never performed. Songwriters such as Miura Yoshiko, Aki Yōko, and Matsumiya Kyōko wrote numerous hits for female singers in the late 1970s and 1980s. Their participation in the production process impacted the images of many female singers. For example, when Yamaguchi Momoe was allowed to choose the lyricists for her songs, Aki wrote many of her lyrics, beginning with "Yokosuka Story" (1976). These songs transformed Yamaguchi's image from an objectified and sexualized girl to a self-assured woman—a change that both Yamaguchi and her audience embraced (Tsutsumi 2000, 49).

As a popular and sought-after songwriter since her breakthrough in 1975, Yuming was a prime example of this change in kayōkyoku. Her success in kayōkyoku songwriting is illustrated not only by the songs on *The 14th Moon* but also by her songs from the 1980s, which have been regarded as indispensable for the development of the genre. In 1981, lyricist and producer Matsumoto Takashi (a former member of Happy End) asked Yuming to compose songs for idol singer Matsuda Seiko in the hope of raising her popularity among female audiences, who largely disliked Matsuda's image as a cute and helpless girl (*burikko*) (Ogawa 1988, 153; Yanagisawa 2011, 197). Yuming's hit songs for Matsuda, such as "Red Sweet Pea" (Akai suītopī, 1982) and "Tanned Mermaid" (Komugi-iro no māmeido, 1982), helped raise her to nationwide popularity and made her one of the most successful singers of the 1980s (Ogura 1989, 182–4).

Following this example, many idol producers began to hire more women songwriters to write songs that would appeal to the broadest possible audience (Ogawa 1988, 154–5). This approach was successful: Takeuchi Mariya's songs for Kawai Naoko and Okada Yukiko are now considered classics of idol pop, and several writers have even credited the idol boom of the 1980s to women's songwriting skills, due to a "feminine" stance that appealed to female audiences (Nagai 2013, 141). In other words, the music industry was starting to acknowledge both the value of female creators and the importance of female audiences.

In the wake of these developments, women also became more involved in other aspects of production. Singer-songwriters such as Yoshida Minako and Ozaki Amii, who sang background vocals on *The 14th Moon*, later produced not only their own albums but also those of younger singer-songwriters and kayōkyoku singers, such as Iijima Mari and Hayami Yū. With more active involvement of women in production and marketing positions, a greater variety of women's images were projected in Japanese popular music (Igarashi 1999, 105). Their legacy can be witnessed in the success of the next generation of female J-pop musicians, such as Utada Hikaru and Shiina Ringo, whom music critic Take Hideki has dubbed "the Yumings of the 1990s" (Take 1999, 317).

With its new expressions of authenticity and portrayal of independent heroines, *The 14th Moon* represents this broader trend in which women's roles in popular music, lyrics, and production became increasingly diverse with the influx of women creators. As Yuming and other female singer-songwriters emphasized their creativity, their individualism contributed to broader changes taking place in popular media and positioned Yuming's work in between women's media and the mainstream media. In this respect, Yuming embodied a liberal feminist trend within the music industry. Perhaps these aspects encouraged Yuming to say that her work in the 1970s was "backstage version of women's liberation" (Chikushi 1984, 54).

The image of the soaring woman (although the term is not used anymore) has stayed with Yuming across the decades after *The 14th Moon*. When the popular weekly tabloid *Shūkan gendai* compiled a ranking of Japan's "true geniuses" in late 2019 based on the criteria of intelligence, determination, sensibility, and capability, Yuming and Nakajima Miyuki were the only women included in the top ten (Shūkan gendai 2020). The result highlights the continuing cultural impact of women singer-songwriters and their importance as examples. But whereas the discussion above has focused on Yuming's position as a female musician, there is yet another transformation in Japanese popular music history that *The 14th Moon* reflects. To address this transformation, we turn to the legacy of the album.

6 Musical Legacies

Pop songs only become complete when the listener hears it. They grow from being linked to that person's memories. So what you presented could grow without limits, each sound spreading as far and wide as the number of people who listened to it.

– YUMING (MATSUTŌYA 2011, 35)

In October 2020, the insurance company Sony Assurance conducted a survey about driving habits in Japan (Sony Sonpo 2020). While most questions dealt with topics such as the respondents' monthly budget for driving, favorite car brand, and opinions on how to prevent road rage, the survey also included a question about their favorite music while driving on a date. With 1,000 respondents aged from eighteen to fifty-nine, the replies obviously saw wide variation, especially since the questionnaire did not give ready alternatives to choose from. Still, the song that ranked number one was overwhelmingly clear. It was "Chuo Freeway."[1]

This result is remarkable, given that the survey was taken more than forty years after the release of *The 14th Moon*. Not even the oldest respondents possessed a driver's license when the album was released! The result demonstrates how classic "Chuo Freeway" has become among Yuming's songs.[2] However, I would argue that its continuing popularity also reflects the significance of *The 14th Moon* in her discography. While the album did not produce pop standards with the ubiquity of "Graduation Photograph" (1975) and "Lipstick Message" (1975), several of its songs have enjoyed continued popularity.

To begin with, almost every song on the album has been covered by prominent musicians, ranging from singer-songwriter Cocco and pop diva Hirahara Ayaka to the all-male rock band Spitz.[3] These musicians represent not only different genres, genders, and generations—many of them were not even born when the album was released—but also different nationalities. "Chuo Freeway" has been covered by foreign musicians in English (by Janis Siegel, A.S.A.P., and Swing Out Sister), French (by Carole Serrat), and Portuguese (by Tatiana). "In the Morning Light" has been recorded in English by the jazz singer Patti Austin, and the Ventures have released an instrumental cover of "The 14th Moon" on their tribute album, *The Ventures Play Yuming* (2013).

Furthermore, many of the songs have been used in television shows. The most prominent example is *Lipstick Message* (Rūju no dengon), a drama series aired by the TBS network in 1991. Each of the twenty-six episodes was based on a song by Yuming, three of these being from *The 14th Moon*.[4] Apart from television, songs on the album have also been used in films and various crossover projects. Director Iwai Shunji used "Like Nothing Ever Happened" in *A Bride for Rip Van Winkle* (2016), and in 2017, the Imperial Theater in Tokyo launched a stage performance based on "In the Morning Light," starring the popular male actor Terawaki Yasufumi and the female idol Miyazawa Sae.

These examples demonstrate that *The 14th Moon* has remained a noteworthy album during the four decades following its release. What is the secret to its longevity? The album's stylistic variety likely appealed to listeners with different musical preferences. But a further reason may be in the way that the album laid the groundwork for later genres of Japanese popular music. "Chuo Freeway" in particular anticipated several trends and laid the groundwork for later genres of Japanese popular music.

From New Music to City Pop and J-pop

After being a housewife for over a year, Yuming made her comeback as a singer-songwriter with her fifth solo album *Linnet* (Benisuzume) in March 1978.[5] The album departed from her earlier work through its focus on acoustic sounds and influence from Latin music genres. Explaining that she wished to "smash the sweet pop sound" of her earlier albums, Yuming saw this stylistic departure as symbolizing the launch of her "Matsutōya Yumi period" (Matsutōya 1984, 139–40). But the relatively subdued *Linnet* was not what audiences anticipated. The most critical voices declared the album as "the end" for Yuming, also partly blaming Matsutōya Masataka for "bad production" (Matsutōya 2016, 89).

At the time *Linnet* was released, Japanese women musicians rarely continued their earlier successes after they were married. The criticism at Yuming's comeback could suggest that she had violated social rules for women: instead of focusing on her duties as a housewife, she returned to public working life and even publicly declared that she "does not need" children (Shūkan myōjō 1978a, 35). However, locating the album's negative reception in gender norms is speculative, as it may well be that *Linnet* simply did not meet expectations for a new Yuming album. Matsutōya Masataka later explained that the two analyzed the situation and decided to take a "step back" toward the styles of *Cobalt Hour* and *The 14th Moon* but with a stronger emphasis on pop sounds. As a result of this decision came Yuming's sixth studio album, *Streamline '80* (Ryūsenkei '80, 1978), which Masataka characterized with three words: "Pop! Pop! Pop!" (Matsutōya 2016, 90).

Pop was apparently what the audience expected from Yuming: *Streamline '80* was welcomed with almost the same excitement as Yuming's earlier work. Soon after its release, a newspaper article enthusiastically declared that the album was leading Japan to the 1980s on the "Yuming express" (Asahi shinbun 1978, 12). Although not a commercial success of the scale of *Cobalt Hour* and *The 14th Moon*, *Streamline '80* nevertheless paved the way to the second Yuming boom of the 1980s and secured her position as an iconic pop-culture symbol of the time (Yanagisawa 2011). Thus, Yuming's "step back" to the styles of *Cobalt Hour* and *The 14th Moon* actually became a "step forward" and marked her comeback as one of the most prominent Japanese musicians.

The release of *Streamline '80* in 1978 coincided with music journalist Tōno Kiyokazu's classification of Yuming's work as "City Music" (*shiti myūjikku*). Explaining that City Music is essentially New Music with a "city" feel, Tōno concluded that the phrase describes a "feeling" rather than a strictly defined musical genre (Tōno 2006, 58). Nevertheless, this "feeling" anticipated the emergence of a new genre name that came to dominate Japanese popular music by singer-songwriters in the early 1980s: City Pop (*shiti poppu*).

By that time, many critics saw that New Music had become "dangerously close" to the kayōkyoku industry (Shūkan heibon 1978, 51). Not only did New Music artists increasingly collaborate with the industry as songwriters and musicians, but kayōkyoku production also began to introduce its own singer-songwriters whose public images were overseen by their management (Lehtonen 2021, 121). In other words, New Music, which had originally been positioned as an "artistic" and "authentic" alternative to kayōkyoku, had become institutionalized in the entertainment industry. Many singer-songwriters were also appearing regularly on television programs that aimed to bridge the gap between New Music and kayōkyoku, such as *Cocky Pop*. This was a notable difference from earlier singer-songwriters, who had shunned performances on television.

For listeners and musicians who wanted to hold on to the singer-songwriter's image of authenticity, this level of integration was too much. In the same way that New Music originally supplanted folk and rock as the primary "authentic" genre, City Pop was coined to represent a fresher and arguably more polished alternative in Japanese music emphasizing performers' authorship (Kimura 2020, 8). New Music gradually merged with kayōkyoku and fell out of use as a term around 1982 (Take 1999, 235), and the work of countless New Music singer-songwriters like Yuming, Takeuchi Mariya, and Yamashita Tatsurō were classified as City Pop in the 1980s.

Based on this way of presentation, the change from New Music to City Pop may appear as a smooth and natural development. But New Music and City Pop have many musical elements and personnel in common, and as such, it is difficult to distinguish between the two. Take, for example, Takeuchi Mariya. Her name has become virtually synonymous with City Pop, especially after the explosive popularity of her song "Plastic Love" (1984) on YouTube in 2017 accelerated an international City Pop revival. Yet she constantly performed in kayōkyoku shows in the late 1970s, and in the early 1980s, the media specifically characterized her as a New Music singer-songwriter (Shūkan heibon 1981, 145). Attempts at defining City Pop also tend to echo earlier descriptions of New Music. Music journalist Kimura Yutaka defines City Pop as "urban pop for city dwellers" and describes the genre as music that is based on stylistic diversity and characterized by its "city" sound, apolitical lyrics, and musicians who were city dwellers (Kimura 2020, 8–9; Rekōdo korekutāzu 2020, 30–6). This discussion is almost identical with the characterizations that were already invoked about Yuming's work in the mid-1970s (Chapter 3).

In fact, many recent Japanese disc guides and music histories date the beginning of City Pop to the early 1970s, suggesting that the genre overlaps with New Music and aligns with Tōno's definition of "City Music" (Rekōdo korekutāzu 2020). Many of Yuming's songs, before and after *The 14th Moon*, are regularly included in Japanese "best of" discographies of City Pop, although it was only in 1981 that the term "City Pop" was used by the Japanese music press (Sommet 2020, 26). Like many genre names, "City Pop" was a marketers' and journalists' term attached long after the inception of the genre, in this case to categorize those musicians that incorporated "city" themes to their music.

This ambiguity may seem puzzling to anyone who has encountered City Pop through its international revival and the influx of foreign fans. After all, a recent survey indicates that this revival tends to view City Pop as 1980s' Japanese popular music characterized by certain stylistic qualities that align with trends in international popular music at that time, such as jazz harmonies, funk, R&B, disco, and soul, with prominent drums and synthesizers (cf. Kimura 2020, 8; Sommet 2020, 21). But definitions of City Pop in Japan and Western discourse in fact differ from each other. By focusing on sound and musical style, the international definition does not distinguish productional differences or the more specific "city" aspects of 1970s' music. For example, many foreign listeners include several kayōkyoku and idol singers in "Japanese City Pop," although they would not have aligned with the hip image of the genre in the 1980s (Sommet & Katō 2021).

Because of these ambiguities, Moritz Sommet suggests that City Pop should be discerned from an intermedial viewpoint. According to his analysis, City Pop is defined by the records' jackets highlighting cosmopolitan imagery, musical styles that drew on trends in popular music in the United States, and lyrics that "deal with summertime, beaches, holiday resorts and leisurely drives along the coast, with a lesser emphasis given to big city themes" (Sommet 2020, 22).[6] These themes were pictured in the covers and inserts of City Pop albums, which tended to have a "transnational and 'Americanized' flavor," even when depicting Japanese cityscape (Sommet 2020, 22). Often listened to on Walkmans and car stereos, many City

Pop songs were written in a style that made them suitable for "background music" while on the move (Sommet 2020, 22–3).

It is easy to notice that *The 14th Moon* echoes Sommet's characterizations of City Pop. From the driving dates in "The 14th Moon" and "Chuo Freeway" to the beach life in "Sun Shower" and the holiday resort in "A Summer Place," many songs on the album feature the core landscapes of Sommet's characterization. These elements also reflected the prosperity originally associated with New Music: holiday resorts and cars in City Pop symbolized an aspirational lifestyle for an increasingly affluent Japan in the 1970s and 1980s.[7] The album also resonates with the observation about an "Americanized flavor": music writer Ōta Shōichi has argued that despite its references to locations in Tokyo, "Chuo Freeway" represents a "virtual America within Japan" (Ōta 2013, 136).[8] Also the idea about City Pop as "background music" aligns with Yuming's characterization of her work (Heibon 1976, 151). A further link with City Pop is the album's musicians and backup singers, of whom Ōnuki Taeko and Yamashita Tatsurō are often listed among the most prominent City Pop artists.

Furthermore, several recent City Pop guides in Japan include *The 14th Moon* and feature it on their cover (e.g., Kimura 2020). In one of these guides, "Chuo Freeway" was even ranked fourth among best City Pop songs of the 1970s (Rekōdo korekutāzu 2020, 45). Music journalist Makaino Motohiro praises the newness of the City-Pop qualities of the song at that time:

> An important point about the concept of City Pop is the viewpoint of the *suburb*. City Pop is not only the music of the city, but also of the people who come from outside

the city, either to commute to work or to have fun […];
they are certainly city dwellers. "Chuo Freeway" sings about
movement between the city and the suburb, and its use of
a car for transportation was also novel [in popular songs].
[…] [Expressing] the life of the contemporary middle class is
unmistakably City Pop. (Rekōdo korekutāzu 2020, 45)

These observations may seem to contradict my earlier
definition of *The 14th Moon* as a quintessential New Music
album. However, this just goes to show how *The 14th Moon*
challenges simplistic genre definitions and anticipated
themes that were to dominate Japanese popular music in
the following years. Although the album differs in musical
characteristics from how foreign audiences in particular have
imagined City Pop, these became much more prominent in
Yuming's work of the 1980s. *SURF & SNOW* (1980) in particular
fits the City Pop moniker, according to recent international
perceptions. The album not only refers to typical City Pop
themes (surfing, skiing, resort life, discotheques) but also
emphasizes synthesizers and drums more than did Yuming's
albums of the 1970s. *SURF & SNOW* also marked the beginning
of the "second Yuming boom" that made her a popular City
Pop artist, a symbol of bubble-economy Japan, and a role
model for working women (Yanagisawa 2011, 207–9).

But even if *The 14th Moon* is not a full-fledged City Pop
album in this context, it could certainly be understood as a
bridge between New Music and 1980s' City Pop. Its generic
hybridity is also applicable to Yuming's broader position in
Japanese popular music, as the variety of Yuming's output
makes it virtually impossible to pin her work to an individual

genre. Yuming was not only among the instigators of both New Music and City Pop, but also among the first artists classified as J-pop in the late 1980s when the term was coined (Ugaya 2005, 8). At the same time, her songs written for other singers represent and converge with kayōkyoku and enka, and she has even written a school song (*kōka*) for a high school in Nagasaki.

These various facets of Yuming's creative output exemplify her stylistic eclecticism and demonstrate her skills in adapting to and foreshadowing changes in the commercial music industry. But her continuing popularity and the variety of her work also demonstrate an ability to express something relevant to listeners from generation to generation. The musical legacy of *The 14th Moon* can be best understood as part of this longer continuum: like Yuming's work at large, its songs cross generic boundaries and attract new audiences even forty years after its release. Therefore, it is not that surprising that "Chuo Freeway" can still be chosen as the best song for a driving date in 2020. Such positive evaluations place *The 14th Moon* in a position similar to its heroines: the album focuses on individual moments, but while doing so, it always remains integrated with the flow of time.

Conclusion

*My ideal is always to stay one step away from completion.
I believe that anything that becomes completed will turn
empty. So, to avoid becoming a full moon myself, it may also
be the time for me to let go of something I no longer need.*
– YUMING (ARAI 1976B, 58)

In 2016, Matsutōya Masataka published a book looking back at his and Yuming's musical journey. Packed with fascinating insights into Japanese popular music of the past decades, the book presents numerous delectable anecdotes and Matsutōya's thoughts about popular music in Japan. Among these, a particularly interesting one is related to how Matsutōya sees music mirroring its time:

> Even if one is not aware of it, the air of the era more or less
> blows through recorded sounds. The music of the 1970s
> has its distinct air, and so does the music of the 80s. With
> this in mind, I always want to make realistic music. I want
> to transform our real emotions of the present moment into
> sound. In my opinion, it's always good if a realistic scene
> emerges when lyrics, singing, melodies, arrangements, and
> performances come together. (Matsutōya 2016, 28–9)

The 14th Moon perfectly encapsulates Matsutōya's observation. It is, in Matsutōya's terms, a "realistic" work that accurately (albeit implicitly) describes its surroundings through musical, visual, and production details. Its descriptive qualities, combined with its stylistic variety and convergence with later genres, have inspired new audiences and musicians and made it representative of New Music. But if New Music is so "realistic," what, in fact, accounts for the "newness" of the genre?

As we saw earlier, both feminism and New Music arose from the same social developments: postwar urbanization and economic growth. Both of them also became major trends in the mid-1970s. But while sharing the same roots, they developed in distinct ways. Whereas women's movements addressed gender inequality issues that had emerged as a by-product of postwar developments, New Music showed women taking more varied roles in an increasingly affluent Japan than those assigned to them by the postwar society. In this respect, the genre became a space for women to express themselves on their own terms—a legacy inherited by women singer-songwriters in City Pop and J-pop.[1] Therefore, it seems natural that New Music has been strongly associated with Yuming. Her image and musical style did not fit into pre-existing models for Japanese musicians but explored new territories with their negotiations of authenticity and authorship for women musicians. Even more importantly, audiences and critics welcomed these explorations with enthusiasm.

The true "newness" of New Music, then, was not in its approach to production or sound neither in its ways of bridging commercialism and artistic integrity. Its novelty was its soaring women: the women singer-songwriters whose work launched a musical decade of women that resulted in some of the most memorable artists in Japanese popular music, such as Nakajima Miyuki, Takeuchi Mariya, and Ōnuki Taeko, who debuted at this time. In this way, the numerous cover versions, also the long-lived popularity of the songs, and the historical canonization of *The 14th Moon* attest to the broader significance of women's creative work in Japanese popular music. It is equally significant that *The 14th Moon* never became a swan song. Instead, the album became a prelude that anticipated what follows.

This brings us back to the moon on the fourteenth night: the time before completion when one is full of anticipation. I have always found Yuming's comment in her essay—quoted at the beginning of this chapter—to be enigmatic. What did she wish to "let go of?" Was it a subtle hint that she had decided to end her career as a singer-songwriter—an intention she did not openly reveal until the 1980s? Did she refer to her marriage, the end of her "Arai Yumi period," as her early work is now known? Or was she stating that she aspired to develop some aspects of her work to avoid repeating herself? To me, all these interpretations would seem equally plausible.

But these questions do not really matter. What matters is everything that followed. *The 14th Moon* is the perfect title for an album that anticipated a long, eventful, and flourishing musical career.

Notes

Introduction

1   The impact of Yuming's debut on Japanese popular music has been elaborated on in Tomisawa (1979, 195–202); Ogawa (1988, 51–3); Fukami (1989, 118–39); Take (1999, 169–73); Bourdaghs (2012, 179–86); Nagai (2013, 6–18); Matsuki (2016); and Mitsui (2020, 169–71), among others.

2   In total, her albums and singles have sold more than forty million copies. At the time of this writing, Yuming has released thirty-nine studio albums, forty-one singles, and nearly 200 songs written for other artists.

3   As a non-Japanese male scholar writing over forty years after the release of *The 14th Moon*, I acknowledge the limitations that my positioning puts on my readings of Yuming's lyrics and understanding of her social position. When discussing Yuming as a female musician, I am especially invested in examining what Japanese women have written about her work.

Chapter 1

1   The most comprehensive account of Yuming's early years is her autobiography *Lipstick Message* (Rūju no dengon), named after one of her most well-known songs (Matsutōya 1984). Virtually all subsequent descriptions of her youth tend to lean on this account. Apart from *Lipstick Message*,

I will also cite several articles dating from the 1970s, where Yuming describes some aspects of her musical background in more detail.

2   Alfa Music was founded as a subsidiary of Toshiba EMI. It became an independent record company as Alfa Records in 1977. In addition to producing, Murai is well-known in Japan for composing the folk group Akai Tori's "Please Give Me Wings" (Tsubasa o kudasai, 1971).

3   Popular music scholar Wajima Yūsuke (2004) has written that Happy End's impact on Japanese music history has often been exaggerated in the hope of legitimizing musical acts and genres with which its members later collaborated.

4   Miyazaki and his producer Suzuki Toshio did not read "Vapor Trail" as a song about suicide, though, but found its lyrics a perfect match for Horikoshi Jirō's pursuit to design the perfect aircraft in *The Wind Rises* (Suzuki & Matsutōya 2013, 56).

5   However, two members play on some tracks of the album: Suzuki Shigeru on the electric guitar and Hosono Haruomi on the steel drum.

6   By the mid-1970s, it had become common for Japanese musicians to record their albums in the United States to bring an international flavor to their work, whereas inviting foreign musicians to Japan was much less common. Matsutōya met Sklar in Seto's concert and requested him to participate in the recordings; Sklar agreed and invited Baird. Sklar was a well-known musician already at that time, having performed with stars such as Carole King, Phil Collins, Olivia Newton-John, and James Taylor. Yuming was to collaborate with Sklar—and other foreign musicians—on many of her later albums.

Chapter 2

1 A few weeks after the release of *The 14th Moon*, Yuming published a photograph and essay collection by the same name (Arai 1976b). Nagahama's photographs in this collection engage with the same interplay, but even more prominently: they range from almost mundane shots about Yuming having a meal to ethereal photographs of her clad in a kimono. Yuming's involvement with fashion became even more conspicuous later: the cover of her seventh album, *OLIVE* (1979), evokes an Italian fashion magazine, and she has published numerous fashionable photograph collections since the 1970s.

2 "In the Morning Light" was written for the trio Hi-Fi Set to perform as the theme song of the film *Glacial River* (Tōga, 1976), whereas "Good Luck and Goodbye" was originally sung by Okazaki Yuki. "A Summer Place" was the theme song of the Isetan department store's summer campaign. "Chuo Freeway" and "Sun Shower" were written for television programs where Yuming herself premiered them, whereas "Late Summer (The Lonely Season)" was the theme song for a television show run by the national broadcasting company NHK.

3 Yuming's songs strongly suggest that their protagonists are women. They use feminine sentence endings such as *no, wa,* and *no yo,* and refer to themselves with the feminine pronouns *watashi* and *atashi*. Yuming typically does not specify the gender of her heroines' love interests. As she is a singer-songwriter who reflects on her lived experiences in her songs (Kitanaka 1979, 42), I have assumed the love interests of her heroines to be men, as most writers about Yuming have (cf. Fukai 1989; Sakai 2013).

4 The title originated from the Japanese film, *Love and Parting in Sri Lanka* (Suri Ranka no ai to wakare, 1976). Yuming took a liking to a line she came across in a movie magazine: "I prefer the moon on the fourteenth night to the full moon. After all, on the fourteenth, there's still a tomorrow" (Arai 1976b, 58).

5 My understanding of the terms verse, chorus, and bridge follow John Covach's definitions. "The 14th Moon" is based on a verse-chorus form (with a pre-chorus here). Several other songs on the album follow an AABA scheme, consisting of a verse performed twice (AA), a bridge (B), and a reprise of the verse (A). As Covach explains: "In an AABA song, the focus of the music is in the verse sections; the bridge exists simply to offer contrast, making the verse seem fresh on its reappearance. In a verse-chorus song, by contrast, the focus of the song is squarely on the chorus" (Covach 2005, 71).

6 By "premodern culture," I refer to the various forms of Japanese culture before 1868, when Japan started a process of modernization based on Western example.

7 Japanese musicians, when entering the global arena, are often expected to represent a markedly "Japanese" quality (defined in terms of "traditional" culture). This expectation typically adheres to notions of "Japanese uniqueness" as articulated by the Japanese discourse known as *Nihonjinron* (cf. Befu 2001). As music scholar Noriko Manabe points out, it is also indicative of a broader issue: that of viewing Japan as a "perpetual Other" for the West (Manabe 2013).

8 The words used in the first verse are: sky-blue (*sorairo*), pale blue (*mizuiro*), deep red (*akane*), and crimson (*kurenai*).

9 One example of this device in Yuming's work is "Logbook" (Kōkai nisshi) on *Cobalt Hour*. Although the Japanese title translates as "logbook" (literally, "voyage log"), the word *kōkai* in the lyrics is written with different characters that change the meaning to "a log of regrets."

10 Literally, they translate as "not saying [it] is [like] a flower" and "wind in willows."

11 These refer to the Tokyo Racetrack in Fuchū and the Suntory Musashino Beer Factory.

12 For example, a "rose losing its color" may represent a woman's fear of her beauty fading with age. I thank Noriko Manabe for suggesting this interpretation.

Chapter 3

1 "Middle-class sound" (*chūsan kaikyū saundo*): Matsutōya (1984, 9–10); "leisure-class sound" (*yūkan kaikyū saundo*): Kamura (1975); "bourgeois" (*burujoa*): Heibon (1976, 151).

2 For more detailed discussions on the social implications of contemporary music production, see Tomisawa (1979); Ogawa (1988); Take (1999); Azami (2004); Stevens (2008); Bourdaghs (2012); and Mitsui (2020). Today, the word kayōkyoku is occasionally used to refer to all postwar Japanese popular music before the emergence of J-pop in the late 1980s, but in the 1970s, it carried a more specific meaning as a production model and as a genre (Lehtonen 2021, 117–9). Another widely used term is *Shōwa kayō*, Shōwa-period (1926–1989) popular songs.

3 Whereas rock and folk were the primary genres emphasizing musical authenticity in the late 1960s and early 1970s, musician-led genres that triumphed in the 1970s and 1980s include New Music and City Pop. All these originally represented an alternative to kayōkyoku but eventually became assimilated by the industry. The division between kayōkyoku and musician-led genres ended in the late 1980s, when the most important dividing line was drawn between "international-style" J-pop and "Japanese-style" enka (Ugaya 2005).

4 Yuming often called folk "4.5 *tatami* mat songs," by which she meant folk lyrics that depict young, poor students, living in cramped rooms and lamenting social injustice (Matsutōya 1984, 9). The protagonist of *Somehow, Crystal* also uses the phrase, the annotator explaining that the term refers to folk songs "smelling of sweat" (Tanaka 1981, 84, 176).

5 The number of people living in cities nearly doubled from 1950 to 1970. In 1950, 38 percent of the Japanese population lived in cities; by 1970, this number had risen to 72 percent (Okamoto 2015, 79).

6 A survey by the national broadcasting company NHK indicated that the tastes and leisure activities of white- and blue-collar workers were no longer remarkably different (NHK 1971). Simultaneously, a quasi-academic discourse called *Nihonjinron* popularized the conception that Japanese culture and all Japanese were connected by a unique "Japaneseness" that was largely defined by equating ethnicity, culture, and nationality with each other (Befu 2001). However, the image of economic and social equality was highly debatable. Economic inequity had in fact increased since the end of the war, and the oil shock of 1973 negatively impacted the life of many Japanese.

7 The term was first used in the *New Music Magazine* in 1969 to refer to contemporary foreign musicians such as the Beatles and Bob Dylan, but it came to signify the Japanese genre around the mid-1970s.

8 For examples, see Aono (1976, 123); Shūkan heibon (1978, 49); Ogawa (1988, 51); Yazawa (1991, 125); Kikuchi (2008, 248); Stevens (2008, 47); Bourdaghs (2012, 179); and Mitsui (2020, 169).

9 Aono (1976); Shūkan heibon (1978); Tomisawa (1979); Kuji (1982); Ogawa (1988, 45–54); Take (1999, 154–65); Azami (2004, 174–9); Stevens (2008, 46–9); smf Bourdaghs (2012, 161–3). Exceptions did naturally exist. For example, singer-songwriter Sada Masashi was classified as New Music but was also known for expressing politically reactionary views in his songs.

10 By contrast, beginning in the late 1970s, Yuming became famous for her practice of releasing two albums every year.

11 For example, Kamura (1975, 209); Shūkan gendai (1976, 169); Shūkan myōjō (1976b, 151); Suzuki (1976, 55); Matsutōya (1977, 95); Tomisawa (1979, 201); and Matsutōya (1984, 132).

12 Yoshida was among the first singer-songwriters who wrote songs for television dramas and commercials while declining performances on television himself. This resulted in a new form of reciprocal marketing. For example, when Yoshida's "Have a Nice Day" (1971) was used in a television commercial for Fuji Film, the commercial also advertised the song and made it a hit (Ogawa 1988, 50).

13 Yuming did occasionally perform in programs where she could sing more than one song and thereby express her musical profile comprehensively. For example, *Seven Star Show*, for which she composed "Chuo Freeway," was over one hour long and gave her plenty of opportunities to demonstrate the different aspects of her musicianship (Suzuki 1976, 57). The stigmatization of television performances among singer-songwriters ended in the 1980s. Yuming eventually made her first appearance in *Kōhaku utagassen* in 2005 and has performed on the show several times thereafter.

Chapter 4

1 In Japanese, *joshi gakusei bōkokuron*. The debate has been comprehensively analyzed by Bullock (2014).

2 The number of women (aged fifteen and over) in the labor force in 1955 was 56.7 percent, whereas in 1965 it was 50.6 percent and in 1975 it was at its lowest at 45.7 percent. The decrease is mainly explained by the increasing number of housewives and female students; in 1975, 68.56 percent of those women not in the labor force were housewives (Statistics Bureau of Japan). The actual number of housewives was somewhat higher than the statistics would suggest, as the numbers for women in the labor force also include professional housewives who only earned extra income for their families in low-paid part-time jobs (Ochiai 1996, 13–14). This practice became increasingly common in the 1970s (Ueno 1988, 176–7).

3 In premodern Japan, *kanpaku* referred to the emperor's "chief adviser," who was the de facto ruler. Sada's song humorously compares the domestic role of the husband to that of the *kanpaku*.

4 For more extensive analyses and examples, see Jugaku (1979); Zettsu (2002); Ogawa (1999); and Yano (2002, 149–52).

5 For similar observations about other media in contemporary Japan, see Muramatsu (2002); Shigematsu (2005); Amano et al. (2009); and Ueno (2012).

6 Very few songs explicitly challenged conventional gender roles, but there are some examples among politically oriented folk songs. Takaishi Tomoya's "Housewife Blues" (Shufu no burūsu, 1968) suggests that the role of a housewife is bound to lead to a life full of disappointments.

7 Arima was invited to write lyrics by her husband, producer and composer Suzuki Jun. Iwatani and Yasui became involved with the kayōkyoku industry as translators of foreign-language lyrics into Japanese but were later commissioned to write their original lyrics.

8 Shimazaki refers to Murasaki Shikibu and Sei Shōnagon, two Heian-period court ladies who significantly impacted Japanese literary culture with their classics, *The Tale of Genji* (Murasaki) and *The Pillow Book* (Sei). Often noted for their different personalities and styles of writing, Shimazaki makes a similar comparison between Yuming and Nakajima.

9 The women's liberation movement addressed a broad array of issues, encompassing women's sexuality, reproduction control, eugenics, migrants' rights, ethnicity, disability, social class, imperialism, militarism, nationalism, and environmental issues (Shigematsu 2012). For accounts on the history and debates of Japanese feminisms, including those that emerged before the 1970s, see Mackie (2003) and Kano (2016).

10 "Toilet" refers to an extreme discourse of the late 1960s, where activist women were called "public toilets" (*benjo*) for men to relieve themselves sexually (Shigematsu 2012, 45).

Chapter 5

1 Marketed as an "impact magazine for businessmen," *Shinpyō* discussed topics such as politics, economy, sports, women, and culture.

2 This result remarkably differs from the situation today, as gender notably segregates the audiences of different genres (Minamida et al. 2019, 73–5).

3 The songs Sakai discusses are "One Afternoon by the Sea" (Umi o miteita gogo) and "You Left Me" (Tabun anata wa mukae ni konai) from *MISSLIM*.

4 Although Yuming's songs in the 1970s were mostly arranged by Matsutōya Masataka, she explained that her husband completes the arrangements according to her wishes and instructions (Ren'ai kajin kenkyūkai 1996, 89–90). Itsuwa mainly arranged her songs herself in the 1970s, and Ozaki arranged hers starting from her third album *Stop Motion* (1978); her previous two albums were arranged by Matsutōya.

5 A fitting example is the all-female punk band, Shonen Knife. Since its debut in 1981, Shonen Knife has challenged stereotypical gender (and racial) representations by combining "cool pop punk sounds with cute lyrics" (McCorkle Okazaki 2021, 7). Numerous examples can also be found from the 2010s; acts like Babymetal, BAND-MAID, and Lovebites have gained popularity among international audiences with their combination of cute visuals and lyrics with heavy rock sounds.

6 Japan's ranking in the same report was also low in preceding years—121st in 2020, 110th in 2018, and 114th in 2017. Japan has constantly ranked lowest among G7 countries; in the 2021 report, the next lowest is Italy, which ranked 63rd.

7 Japanese law does not allow married couples to have different surnames, and most women give up their maiden name when they marry. However, female musicians and other public personas often keep them as their stage names.

8 However, most women returned to singing only after a break, as combining motherhood and professional life was still a taboo. This was exemplified in the case of Agnes Chan, who brought her child to her workplace in 1987, which stirred notable controversy especially among other women (Kano 2016, 126–7).

Chapter 6

1	"Chuo Freeway" got twenty votes. While not such a great number, it clearly surpassed the second song, Arashi's "Happiness" (nine votes) and the three songs that ranked third (eight votes each).

2	In a survey about Yuming's songs by *Aera* magazine in 2009, "Chuo Freeway" ranked fifth—surpassing even such all-time favorites as "Come, Spring" (Haru yo, koi, 1994), "DESTINY" (1979), and "Vapor Trail" (Aera 2009). In a 1988 survey about Yuming's songs for novelists, scriptwriters, and musicians, it ranked number one (Fukami 1989, 8–9).

3	To name but a few, these artists include: Cocco, Haigō Meiko, Hi-Fi Set, Hirahara Ayaka, Imai Miki, Inoue Yōsui, Nomiya Maki, Ōhashi Junko, Shōno Mayo, Spitz, Takagi Ayako, Tendō Yoshimi, and Yaguchi Mari.

4	The songs were "Chuo Freeway" (episode 7), "Good Luck and Goodbye" (episode 9), and "The 14th Moon" (episode 17).

5	To be more precise, Yuming had released two singles and one best-of album while a housewife. Yuming later characterized the best-of album as her "worst work," and the singles were apparently seen as a proof that a second Yuming boom would be impossible (Matsutōya 1984, 132; 139).

6	The quotations are from an unpublished English-language version of the paper.

7   In 1977, Japanese households owned an average of 0.534 cars vs. 1.59 for US households. The number of cars owned in Japan rose 2.5 times from 1965 to 1975, and another 69 percent from 1975 to 1985 (Jidōsha kensa tōroku jōho kyōkai 2019; U.S. Department of Transportation 1980).

8   Note how different this argument is from Uchida Tatsuru's comment about "Chuo Freeway" as analogous to classical Japanese poetry (Chapter 2).

Conclusion

1   In J-pop, this pertains to singer-songwriters such as Utada Hikaru, Shiina Ringo, Onitsuka Chihiro, and aiko. All of them contributed to a new boom of female singer-songwriters in the late 1990s. Unlike female singer-songwriters in the 1970s, neither their emergence coincided with the rise of a feminist movement, nor their music addressed feminist issues. However, their work did inherit the legacy of foregrounding women musicians' individual creativity within the music industry.

Bibliography

Aera 2009. "Intoro o kiku to, dōshite nakeru darō: Yūmin songu no shunkashūtō." *Aera* 22 (16): 54.

Amano, Masako et al. (eds.) 2009. *Shinpen Nihon no feminizumu 7.* Tokyo: Iwanami shoten.

Aono, Motō 1976. "Nyū myūjikku no kishutachi." *Sandē mainichi* 55 (10): 123–5.

Arai, Yumi 1976a. "Kokoro no tobira o tataku messēji." *Seventeen* 9 (7): 54–7.

Arai, Yumi 1976b. *Jūyonbanme no tsuki: The 14th Moon.* Tokyo: Peppu shuppan.

Asahi shinbun 1978. "80nendai e hashiridashita 'Yūmin tokkyū.'" *Asahi shinbun*, December 7: 12.

Asahi shinbun 1980. "Konomarenai tonderu onna." *Asahi shinbun*, November 7: 15.

Azami, Toshio 2004. *Popyurā ongaku wa dare ga tsukuru no ka: Ongaku sangyō no seijigaku.* Tokyo: Keisō shobō.

Befu, Harumi 2001. *Hegemony of Homogeneity: An Anthropological Analysis of Nihonjinron.* Melbourne: Trans Pacific Press.

Bentley, Christa Anne 2018. "'Poet-Composers': Art and Legitimacy in the Singer-Songwriter Movement." In *The Routledge Companion to Popular Music Analysis: Expanding Approaches*, ed. Ciro Scotto, Kenneth Smith, and John Brackett. New York: Routledge, 416–25.

Bourdaghs, Michael K. 2012. *Sayonara Amerika, Sayonara Nippon: A Geopolitical Prehistory of J-Pop.* New York: Columbia University Press.

Bullock, Julia C. 2014. "'Female Students Ruining the Nation': The Debate over Coeducation in Postwar Japan." *U.S.-Japan Women's Journal* 46: 3–23.

Butler, Judith 1999. *Gender Trouble*. Second edition. New York: Routledge.

Chen, Shī Yū [Sy Chen] 2005. *Inpuresario: Seikō ukeoinin*. Tokyo: Daiyamondo-sha.

Chiharu, Chujo and Nobuyo Aizawa 2020. "Women's Movements in 1970s Japan: Transgression and Rejection." In *Engendering Transnational Transgressions*, ed. Eileen Boris, Sandra Trudgen Dawson, and Barbara Molony. London: Routledge, 133–46.

Chikushi, Tetsuya 1984. "Wakamonotachi no kamigami: Matsutōya Yumi." *Asahi Journal* 26 (35): 51–5.

Cogan, Brian and Gina Cogan 2006. "Gender and Authenticity in Japanese Popular Music: 1980–2000." *Popular Music and Society* 29 (1): 69–90.

Covach, John 2005. "Form in Rock Music: A Primer." In *Engaging Music: Essays in Music Analysis*, ed. Deborah Stein. New York and Oxford: Oxford University Press, 65–76.

Dan, Ikuma 1977. "Ii ne ano hito: Matsutōya Yumi." *Asahi shinbun*, January 11 (evening print): 4.

Ehara, Yumiko 1993. "Japanese Feminism in the 1970s and 1980s." *U.S.-Japan Women's Journal* 4: 49–69.

Fukami, Haruka 1989. *Yūmin no toiki*. Tokyo: Mirion shuppan.

Fukushima, Mizuho 2014. "Yūmin no tsumi (Sakai Junko) o yonde." http://mizuhofukushima.blog83.fc2.com/blog-entry-2403.html

Gender Equality Bureau Cabinet Office 2021. *Reiwa 2-nendo danjo-kyōdō sankaku shakai no keisei no jōkyō*. https://www.gendergo.jp/about_danjo/whitepaper/r03/zentai/pdf/r03_genjo.pdf

Gluck, Carol S. 1993. "The Past in the Present." In *Postwar Japan as History*, ed. Andrew Gordon. California: University of California Press, 64–95.

Gordon, Andrew 2005. "Managing the Japanese Household: The New Life Movement in Postwar Japan." In *Gendering Modern*

Japanese History, ed. Barbara Molony and Kathleen Uno. Cambridge and London: Harvard University Press, 423–60.

Hagita, Mitsuo 2018. *Hittokyoku no ryōrinin: Henkyokuka Hagita Mitsuo no jidai*. Tokyo: Rittor Music.

Hase, Masato and Ōta Shōichi (eds.) 2007. *Terebi da yo! Zen'in shūgō*. Tokyo: Seikyūsha.

Heibon 1976. "Fōku shinshiroku: Arai Yumi." *Heibon* 32 (5): 150–1.

Higashi, Yōichi 1981. "Gesuto shinkyoku ga daihitto shiteiru Matsutōya Yumi." *Shūkan heibon* 23 (38): 48–52.

Holt, Fabian 2007. *Genre in Popular Music*. Chicago: The University of Chicago Press.

Igarashi, Tadashi 1999. "Ongaku sangyō ni okeru josei." In *Narihibiku "sei": Nihon no popyurā ongaku to jendā*, ed. Kitagawa Junko. Tokyo: Keisō shōbō, 84–106.

Inoue, Takako 1999. "'Itsudatsu' o enjiru: Onnanoko-bando taiken kara mita 'rokku to sei'." In *Narihibiku "sei"*, ed. Kitagawa Junko. Tokyo: Keisō shōbō, 58–83.

Inoue, Teruko 1981. *Joseigaku to sono shūhen*. Tokyo: Keisō shobō.

Inoue, Teruko 2009. "Media ga josei o tsukuru? Josei ga media o tsukuru?." In *Shinpen Nihon no feminizumu 7*, ed. Amano Masako et al. Tokyo: Iwanami shoten, 2–30.

Jidōsha kensa tōroku jōhō kyōkai 2019. *News Release*. https://www.airia.or.jp/publish/file/r5c6pv000000mhvq-att/r5c6pv000000mhw5.pdf

Jugaku, Akiko 1979. *Nihongo to onna*. Tokyo: Iwanami shoten.

Kamidate, Kazunori 2019. "Takeuchi Mariya. Watashi wa utaite, motomerareru ongaku, jibun ga tsukuritai ongaku no baransu daiji." *Shūkan asahi* 124 (49): 112–15.

Kamura, Masamichi 1975. "Arai Yumi: Shin bun'ya 'Yūkan kaikyū saundo' o umidasu Yūmin." *Shūkan posuto* 7 (48): 207–9.

Kano, Ayako 2016. *Japanese Feminist Debates*. Honolulu: University of Hawai'i Press.

Kano, Ayako 2018. "On Rethinking Japanese Feminisms." In *Rethinking Japanese Feminisms*, ed. Julia C. Bullock, Ayako Kano, and James Welker. Honolulu: University of Hawai'i Press, 267–82.

Katō, Kōichi 1979. "Tonderu onnatachi ga geinōkai o nurikaeru." *Eiga jōhō* 44 (1): 46–7.

Katsura, Sanshi 1976. "Katsura Sanshi no oyoyo taiwa (4): Arai Yumi." *Mimi* 2 (2): 80–4.

Kearney, Mary Celeste 2017. *Gender and Rock*. New York: Oxford University Press.

Kikuchi, Kiyomaro 2008. *Nihon ryūkōka hensenshi*. Tokyo: Ronsōsha.

Kimura, Yutaka 2020. *Japanese City Pop Revisited*. Tokyo: Shinkō myūjikku.

Kirarasha 2003. *Matsutōya Yumi: Yuming*. Tokyo: TOKYO FM shuppan.

Kitagawa, Junko 1999. "Tatakae! Shōnen: Terebi manga shudaika to jendā." In *Narihibiku "sei"*, ed. Kitagawa Junko. Tokyo: Keisō shōbō, 180–210.

Kitanaka, Masakazu 1979. "Za myūjikku pīpuru: Matsutōya Yumi." *Shūkan myōjō* 22 (35): 38–43.

Kobayashi, Akira 2001. *Sasurai*. Tokyo: Shinchōsha.

Komori, Masaki 2011. "Wakamono zasshi to 1970 nendai no Nihon ni okeru 'Amerikanaizēshon' no hen'yō." *Shuppan kenkyū* 42: 47–68.

Kuji, Toshitake 1982. "Ryūkōka no shakaigaku." *Mie daigaku kyōiku gakubu kenkyū kiyō* 33: 19–39.

Lehtonen, Lasse 2021. "Japanese Women Singer-Songwriters of the 1970s: Female Agency, Musical Impact and Social Change." *Popular Music* 40 (1): 114–38.

Lieb, Kristin J. 2013. *Gender, Branding, and the Modern Music Industry*. New York: Routledge.

Machin, David 2010. *Analysing Popular Music*. Los Angeles: SAGE.

Mackie, Vera 2003. *Feminism in Modern Japan*. Cambridge: Cambridge University Press.

Manabe, Noriko 2013. "Representing Japan: Japanese Hip-Hop DJs, the Global Stage, and Defining a 'National' Style." *Popular Music* 32 (1): 35–50.

Matsuki, Naoya 2016. *"Arufa no densetsu" sakkyokuka Murai Kunihiko no jidai*. Tokyo: Kawade shobō shinsha.

Matsutōya, Masataka 2016. *Boku no ongaku kyaria zenbu hanashimasu*. Tokyo: Shinchōsha.

Matsutōya, Yumi 1977. "Asuterikkuna kōi." *Gendaishi techō* 20 (10): 94–5.

Matsutōya, Yumi 1984. *Rūju no dengon*. Tokyo: Kadokawa shoten.

Matsutōya, Yumi 2011. *Matsutōya Yumi 1972–2011 foto sutōrī*. Tokyo: Shūeisha.

Matsutōya, Yumi and Michishita Kyōko 1979. "Onna o shiboru karakuri ni damasarenai tame ni." *Shinpyō* 26 (9): 106–16.

Mayhew, Emma 1999. "Women in Popular Music and the Construction of 'Authenticity.'" *Journal of Interdisciplinary Gender Studies* 4 (1): 63–81.

McClary, Susan 2002. *Feminine Endings: Music, Gender, and Sexuality*. Minneapolis and London: University of Minnesota Press.

McCorkle Okazaki, Brooke 2021. *Shonen Knife's Happy Hour*. New York: Bloomsbury Academic.

Mimi 1977. "Nyū myūjikku suta melban." *Mimi* 3 (3): 65–71.

Minamida, Katsuya et al. 2019. *Ongakuka shakai no genzai: Tōkei dēta de miru popyurā ongaku*. Tokyo: Shin'yōsha.

Ministry of Health, Labour and Welfare 2015. "Sengyō shufu setai to tomobataraki setai no suii." https://www.mhlw. go.jp/file/05-Shingikai-11201000-Roudoukijunkyoku-Soumuka/0000118655.pdf

Mitsui, Tōru 2020. *Popular Music in Japan: Transformation Inspired by the West*. New York: Bloomsbury Academic.

Murai, Kunihiko 2018. *Murai Kunihiko no LA nikki*. Tokyo: Rittor Music.

Muramatsu, Yasuko 2002. "Gender Construction through Interactions between the Media and Audience in Japan." *International Journal of Japanese Sociology* 11: 72–87.

Music Life 1972. "Ningen hōmon: Itsuwa Mayumi." *Music Life* 22 (11): 188–9.

Music Life 1974. "Ningen hōmon: Arai Yumi." *Music Life* 24 (5): 196–8.

Myōjō 1977a. "Ā, kekkon! Soshite katachiyaburi no shinkon ryokō!" *Myōjō* 26 (2): 90.

Myōjō 1977b. "Seishun kaigi: Ozaki Ami." *Myōjō* 26 (10): 214–16.

Nagahara, Hiromu 2017. *Tokyo Boogie-Woogie: Japan's Pop Era and Its Discontents*. Cambridge: Harvard University Press.

Nagai, Hideharu (ed.) 2013. *Nihon no josei shingā-songuraitā*. Tokyo: Shinkō myūjikku entateimento.

NHK 1971. *Kokumin seikatsu jikan chōsa*. Tokyo: Nippon hōsō shuppan kyōkai.

NHK 1979. *Zenkoku kokumin-ishiki chōsa*. Tokyo: Nippon hōsō shuppan kyōkai.

Ochiai, Emiko 1996. *The Japanese Family System in Transition*. Tokyo: LCTB International Library Foundation.

Ogawa, Hiroshi 1988. *Ongaku suru shakai*. Tokyo: Keisō shobō.

Ogawa, Hiroshi 1999. "Kayōkyoku no naka no otoko to onna." In *Narihibiku "sei"*, ed. Kitagawa Junko. Tokyo: Keisō Shobō, 211–36.

Ogura, Chikako 1989. *Matsuda Seiko-ron*. Tokyo: Asuka shinsha.

Okamoto, Kohei 2015. "Suburbanization of Tokyo and the Daily Lives of Suburban People." In *The Japanese City*, ed. P. P. Karan and Kristin Stapleton. Kentucky: The University Press of Kentucky, 79–105.

Ōta, Shōichi 2013. *Kōhaku utagassen to Nihonjin.* Tokyo: Chikuma Shobō.

Raud, Rein 1994. *The Role of Poetry in Classical Japanese Literature.* Tallinn: Eesti humanitaarinstituut.

Rekōdo korekutāzu 2020. "Arai Yumi: Chūō furīwei." *Shiti poppu meikyoku besuto 100: 1973–1979. Rekōdo korekutāzu* 39 (6): 45.

Ren'ai kajin kenkyūkai 1996. *Matsutōya Yumi no nazo.* Tokyo: Seikokusha.

Sakai, Junko 2013. *Yūmin no tsumi.* Tokyo: Kōdansha.

Seventeen 1981. "Yūmin daikenkyū." *Seventeen* 14 (51): 52–5.

Shaku, Tesshū, Uchida Tatsuru, and Nakoshi Yasufumi 2010. *Gendaijin no inori.* Tokyo: Sanga.

Shigematsu, Setsu 2005. "Feminism and Media in the Late Twentieth Century." In *Gendering Modern Japanese History*, ed. Barbara Molony and Kathleen Uno. Cambridge and London: Harvard University Press, 555–89.

Shigematsu, Setsu 2012. *Scream from the Shadows: The Women's Liberation Movement in Japan.* Minneapolis: University of Minnesota Press.

Shimazaki, Kyōko 2006. "Yūmin, Miyuki sono jidai: Hataraku onna toshite hashiritsuzukeru megamitachi no kiseki to kiseki." *Aera* 19 (17): 86.

Shiota, Sakiko 2000. *Nihon no shakai seiji to jendā.* Tokyo: Nihon hyōrōsha.

Shūkan gendai 1976. "Fuse Akira yori sugoi onnanoko: '75 rekōdo uriage No. 1 kashu 'Yūmin' Arai Yumitte nan da." *Shūkan gendai* 18 (5): 167–9.

Shūkan gendai 2020. "Ima no Nihonjin de tensaitte ieru no wa dare darō." *Shūkan gendai* 62 (1): 172–7.

Shūkan heibon 1976. "Arai Yumi ga okori no hatsugen: 'Atashi wa kashu wa yamemasen!'" *Shūkan heibon* 18 (27): 42–4.

Shūkan heibon 1978. "Nyū myūjikku tettei kenkyū." *Shūkan heibon* 20 (17): 46–51.

Shūkan heibon 1981. "Takeuchi Mariya ga totsujo kashu kyūgō dengon!" *Shūkan heibon* 23 (36): 143–5.

Shūkan myōjō 1976a. "Arai Yumi, sugoi kasegi to shirarezaru shiseikatsu." *Shūkan myōjō* 19 (10): 47–9.

Shūkan myōjō 1976b. "Sugao no Yūmin ni tatchi!" *Shūkan myōjō* 19 (14): n.p.

Shūkan myōjō 1976c. "Posuto Arai Yumi o ninau shingātachi." *Shūkan myōjō* 19 (26): n.p.

Shūkan myōjō 1978a. "Matsutōya Yumi fusai no bakashi ai seikatsu ga genkai ni." *Shūkan myōjō* 21 (36): 31–5.

Shūkan myōjō 1978b. "Izumo kara deta ongakukai no kyūseishu: Takeuchi Mariya wa wandā ūman da." *Shūkan myōjō* 21 (48): 51–3.

Shūkan myōjō 1982. "Supesharu intabyū 39-kai: Matsutōya Yumi." *Shūkan myōjō* 25 (14): 40–5.

Shūkan yomiuri 1981. "Matsutōya Yumi: Kurisutaru josei to nazasareta sono tōmeido." *Shūkan yomiuri* 40 (11): 164–5.

Smith, Christopher 2020. "Somehow, Dialogic: The Dialogic Self and the Rejection of the Modern in *Nantonaku, kurisutaru.*" *Journal of Japanese Studies* 46 (2): 369–93.

Sommet, Moritz 2020. "Popyurā ongaku janru gainen ni okeru kanmediasei to taiwateki kōchiku: 'Japanīzu shiti poppu' o jirei ni." Japanese translation by Katō Ken. *Handai ongakugakuhō* 16–17: 15–42.

Sommet, Moritz and Katō Ken 2021. "Japanese City Pop Abroad." http://doc.rero.ch/record/330193/files/2021_sommet-kato_japanese_city_pop_abroad.pdf

Sony Sonpo 2020. "2020nen zenkoku kāraifu jitsunō chōsa." https://from.sonysonpo.co.jp/topics/pr/2020/12/20201214_01.html

Stanlaw, James 2000. "'Open Your File, Open Your Mind': Women, English, and Changing Roles and Voices in Japanese Popular

Music." In *Japan Pop! Inside the World of Japanese Popular Culture*, ed. Timothy J. Craig. New York: M. E. Sharpe, 75–100.

Statistics Bureau of Japan n.d. "Historical Data 2: Population Aged 15 Years Old and over by Labour Force Status – Whole Japan." https://www.stat.go.jp/data/roudou/longtime/zuhyou/lt02.xlsx

Steel, Gill (ed.) 2019. *Beyond the Gender Gap in Japan*. Michigan: University of Michigan Press.

Stevens, Carolyn S. 2008. *Japanese Popular Music: Culture, Authenticity, and Power*. New York: Routledge.

Suzuki, Naruhiko 1976. "Hitto o tobashitsuzukeru Arai Yumi." *Shūkan heibon* 18 (17): 54–8.

Suzuki, Toshio and Matsutōya Yumi 2013. "Matsutōya Yumi x Suzuki Toshio: Nihon no koi to, Yūmin, Jiburi to." *Neppū: Sutajio Jiburi kōkishin* 11 (3): 51–7.

Take, Hideki 1999. *Yomu J-Pop: Shiteki zenshi*. Tokyo: Tokuma shoten.

Takechi, Yūko 2005. "Gakki no jendā sutereotaipu." *Ongaku kyōikugaku* 35 (1): 1–8.

Tanaka, Yasuo 1981. *Nantonaku, kurisutaru*. Tokyo: Kawade shobō shinsha.

Teruoka, Yasutaka 1962. "Joshigakuseiyo ni habakaru: Kanojora no mokuteki wa nani ka." *Fujin kōron* 47 (3): 277–81.

Tokita, Alison 2010. "The Piano and Cultural Modernity in East Asia." In *Philosophical and Cultural Theories of Music*, ed. Eduardo de la Fuente and Peter Murphy. Leiden: Brill, 221–42.

Tomisawa, Issei 1976. "Yūmin daihyakka." *Heibon panchi* 13 (16): 87–94.

Tomisawa, Issei 1979. *Nyū myūjikku no shōgeki*. Tokyo: Kyōdō tsūshinsha.

Tōno, Kiyokazu 2006. "Shiti myūjikkutte nani?" In *Japanese City Pop*, ed. Kimura Yutaka. Tokyo: Shinkō myūjikku entateimento, 58–61.

Tsurumi, Shunsuke 1984. *Sengo Nihon no taishū bunkashi*. Tokyo: Iwanami shoten.

Tsutsumi, Masashi 2000. "21seiki ni nokoshitai meiban." *The Ichiban*, January 17: 49.

U.S. Department of Transportation 1980. *1977 Nationwide Personal Transportation Study: Household Vehicle Ownership.* https://rosap.ntl.bts.gov/view/dot/5820

Ueno, Chizuko 1988. "The Japanese Women's Movement." In *Modernization and Beyond: The Japanese Trajectory*, ed. Gavan McCormack and Yoshio Sugimoto. Cambridge: Cambridge University Press, 167–85.

Ueno, Chizuko 2009. *The Modern Family in Japan: Its Rise and Fall*. Melbourne: Trans Pacific Press.

Ueno, Chizuko 2012. *Sekushi gyaru no daikenkyū*. Tokyo: Iwanami shoten.

Ugaya, Hiromichi 2005. *J poppu to wa nani ka*. Tokyo: Iwanami shoten.

Wajima, Yūsuke 2004. "'Happii endo shinwa' no kōchiku: Nyū myūjikku, Shibuya-kei, Nihongo rokku." *Yurīka* 36 (9): 180–92.

Warwick, Jacqueline 2007. *Girl Groups, Girl Culture: Popular Music and Identity in the 1960s*. New York: Routledge.

World Economic Forum 2021. *Global Gender Gap Report 2021*. http://www3.weforum.org/docs/WEF_GGGR_2021.pdf

Yamada, Toshihiro 2014. *Ano kashi wa, naze kokoro ni nokoru no ka: J poppu no Nihongoryoku*. Tokyo: Shōdensha.

Yanagisawa, Takeshi 2011. "Jidai o tsukutta onna 1: Matsutōya Yumi." *Bungei shunjū* 89 (3): 196–212.

Yano, Christine R. 2002. *Tears of Longing: Nostalgia and the Nation in Japanese Popular Song*. Cambridge: Harvard University Asia Center.

Yazawa, Kan 1991. "'Dokudan to henken' no hayariuta 50nen shishi, 23." *Asu no nōson* 204: 122–5.

Yomiuri shinbun 1974. "Josei fōkusongu, yonmai no LP." *Yomiuri shinbun*, January 11: 5.

Yoshida, Kaori 1977. "Arai Yumi o tōshite miru atarashii seikatsu no kachikan: Kakoi no naka no shiawase ga miru yume." *Seishōnen mondai* 24 (8): 14–20.

Zettsu, Tomoyuki 2002. *Dō ni mo tomaranai kayōkyoku: 70nendai no jendā*. Tokyo: Shōbunsha.

Index

Index